EASY TO MAKE
MORE PRETTY THINGS

EASY TO MAKE

MORE PRETTY THINGS

Hilary More

ANAYA PUBLISHERS LTD LONDON

First published in Great Britain in 1992
by Anaya Publishers Ltd, Strode House, 44–50 Osnaburgh Street,
London NW1 3ND

Editor Eve Harlow
Designed by Design 23
Photographer Di Lewis
Illustrator Sharon Forbes-Gower
Artwork by Design 23

British Library Cataloguing in Publication Data

More, Hilary
More Pretty Things. – (Easy to make)
1. Handicrafts
I. Title II. Series
745.59
ISBN 1 85470-089-8

Typeset by Servis Filmsetting Ltd, Manchester, UK
Colour reproduction by Columbia Offset, Singapore
Produced by Mandarin Offset.
Printed and bound in Hong Kong.

CONTENTS

Introduction

Simple techniques and easy methods mean that everyone – even beginners – will succeed with the projects in this book. And there is something for everyone regardless of your expertise.

Everyone loves to receive a hand-made gift because it means that the giver has taken the time and effort to make something that is both special and unique. If you are thinking of making a gift for someone, then this book is for you and you will find a present for every occasion. You need no special skills and little equipment, other than the basic things you already have in your home, to make the pretty things in these pages. Most of them need only a small amount of fabric, card or paper and there is a wide choice of gifts for men, women and children.

Of course, the projects need not be made as gifts. The designs will probably appeal to you as things you want to make for yourself, or for your home.

In the first chapter, all the projects are no-sew crafts. Here, you will discover how to construct an amusing flower clock, make some smart buttons and decorate your summer shoes. There are things made from natural materials – pressed flowers decorating a trinket box and an autumnal dried flower tree. I have included some pretty furnishings for the home too – how to cover flower pots with fabric, a flower design to paint on a lampshade and some pretty painted baskets trimmed with stiffened fabric bows in which you can display your dried flowers all year round.

The second section is called
Needlecrafts and this is especially for
everyone who likes to sew. Here you will
discover how to create a smart kitchen
set, make an appliqué tablecloth and
napkins or sew some handy roll-mats for
summer picnics. There are some projects
which will make ideal gifts – such as a
delightful baby bib that squeaks, pretty
slippers in a travel bag, a dressing table
set and, for a homemaker, a smart set of
accessories for the kitchen. There is also
a special Christmas stocking that is sure
to become a family favourite for years to
come.

Finally, the chapter entitled Better
Techniques reminds you of sewing skills
and craft techniques and is a constant
reference for the various methods used in
this book. I recommend that you glance
through this chapter first before starting
on any of the projects.

So, sit and quietly turn the colourful
pages of this book and decide which of
these pretty things appeal to you,
knowing that they will also be welcomed
by the people you care about. Then you
will be ready to create gifts and
accessories for your home that will be
treasured for years to come.

ONE

No-sew Crafts

Flower time

Fantasy time – a flower which can also tell the time. Cut from a cork tile and covered with felt petals this clock has ladybird numbers and filigree hands.

Materials
Cork tile, 12in (30cm) square
Yellow felt, 12in (30cm) square
Oddments of orange and red felts
Pair of clock hands and movement
Few red and black beads
4 ladybird buttons
Craftweight interfacing, 12in (30cm) square
Fabric adhesive
Sharp craft knife

Preparation
1 Draw the pattern for the flower from the graph pattern (scale 1 sq = 1in (2.5cm)). Cut out the pattern and trace down on to the back of the cork tile. Carefully cut out the flower shape.

2 From the pattern trace off each petal, making each one slightly larger along the side edges. Cut 5 petals from yellow felt.

Making the clock
3 Stick a circle of interfacing over the right side of the cork tile flower shape. Turn the tile over and trim the interfacing along the edges of the cork flower.

4 Stick the felt petals in place, overlapping them.

5 Using the paper pattern, cut the larger central circle from orange felt using pinking shears. Cut the smaller circle from red felt, again using pinking shears. Stick the circles in place, one on top of the other.

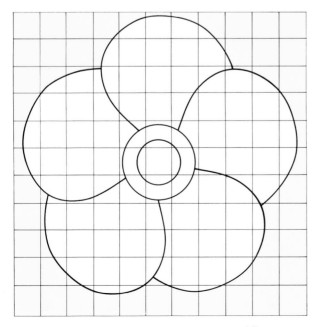

Scale 1 sq = 1in (2.5cm)

6 Drill through the centre of the flower shape and fix the hands in place, with the clock movement on the wrong side, following the manufacturers' instructions.

7 Stick beads along the edges of the petals and in between, alternating red and black (see picture).

8 Make an indentation at the 12, 6, 9 and 3 o'clock positions using a knife tip. Stick 4 ladybird buttons in place.

Glue the overlapping felt petals to the interfacing side of the cork tile

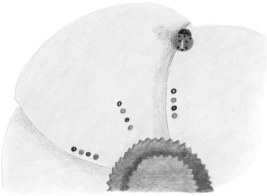

Glue the ladybird buttons in place at 12, 3, 6 and 9

Clever candlesticks

Flour, salt and water mixed together make a pliable dough which you can use to model these pretty candle holders.

Materials
4oz (100g) of plain flour
3oz (75g) of salt
Hot water
10 cloves
Watercolour paints; brush
Spray varnish

Preparation
1 Dissolve the salt in a little hot water. Add cold water. Mix into the flour to make a moist dough. (Add more water if necessary.) Knead the dough well until it is smooth and elastic. Place on a lightly floured board.

Making the apple candlestick
2 Roll out a small amount of dough and, using a cutter (or a cup or mug as a template) cut out a circle, large enough to fit a 2in (5cm)-diameter candle plus an edge. Place the circle of dough on a baking sheet. Hand-roll 2 pieces into thin 'sausages', long enough to fit round the

circumference of the circle. Twist them together. Fix the twisted strips round the circle with a little water, trimming the ends so that they fit together.

3 Roll 10 dough balls the size of marbles for apples. Fit a clove into one end for the stalk. Roll out more dough and cut out 15 tiny leaves. Moisten the leaves and apples and arrange the apples in evenly-spaced pairs, round the twisted edge, each with 3 leaves.

4 Bake the dough model in a cool oven – 110°C (gas mark ¼), until baked hard. Remove from the oven and leave for a few days to dry out completely.

Cut leaves from rolled dough using a sharp knife

Twist strips of dough together to fit round the base

Push cloves into the dough balls for apples

5 Paint the apples red and the leaves green. Leave to dry. When dry, spray varnish all over the candlestick.

Flower candlestick
6 Make up more salt dough in the same way as for the apple candlestick. Roll out the dough, cut petals and make up 10 roses.

7 Form a base in the same way as before. Cut out leaves, moisten with water and fix them, overlapping, all round the base. Arrange the roses.

8 Bake the dough candlestick as before. Paint the leaves green and roses mauve and pink. Leave to dry. Spray with varnish.

Dancing feet

Give a plain pair of canvas shoes a party look with some individual decorations. Whether you prefer beads or shells your shoes will be unique.

Materials
Pair of plain-coloured canvas shoes
Selection of shells
Clear adhesive
42 medium-sized turquoise beads, 46
   small white beads,
2 green, 2 white plastic leaves
4 pink plastic trumpet flowers
Matching sewing threads
Fabric adhesive or Superglue

Preparation
1 Fill the toe end of the shoes with tissue paper to hold the shape while you add the decorations.

2 **Shell shoes:** Carefully stick each shell in position, working both shoes at the same time so that they match. Leave to dry.

3 **Beaded shoes:** String alternate turquoise and white beads on thread to fit round the front of the shoe. Tie a knot on the end of a second piece of thread. Couch between the beads. Finish with a double backstitch.

4 Thread trumpet-shaped flowers and leaves with 2 white beads to decorate the shoes' centre fronts.

5 At the back, make a loop from 3 turquoise and 4 white beads.

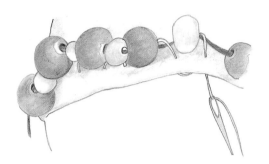

Using a second thread, couch down between each bead

Thread on the beads and catch the thread into the back of the shoe to make a loop

Paint jobs
Summer shoes can also be decorated with painted designs. Some plastic-based colours are available in squeeze bottles and tubes – you just apply the patterns in squirls and blobs and leave to dry. Fluorescent and glitter paints are ideal for putting designs on disco boots and shoes. Sequins can be stuck on for sparkle.

Buttoned up

Brighten up your casual clothes with a set of flower buttons. They're fun to make and fun to wear so just pick your favourite flowers and get rolling. Children will love them!

Materials
Low-bake modelling clay in red, pink, white, green, yellow, orange and blue
Craft knife
Large needle
Rolling pin
Plastic pastry board

Preparation
1 Make a card template of a leaf by drawing round a small real leaf on thin card; carefully cut out.

2 Mix some green and white clay by twisting and rolling them together to marbled green.

Making the leaves
3 Roll out the clay to a thickness of about ⅛in (3mm). Place the template on the clay and, using a craft knife, cut round. Make as many leaves as you require.

4 For a realistic touch, press the real leaf on to the shape, so that the veined structure of the leaf is transferred to the surface of the clay. Use the large needle to make 2 holes in the centre of each leaf.

5 Place the leaves on a sheet of grease-proof paper on a baking tray. Bake at 140°C (gas mark 1) for 20–30 minutes.

Making the flowers
6 **Tulips:** Draw a tulip shape on thin card (refer to the diagram for the shape). Cut out for a template.

7 Mix red and a little orange clay together to give a marbled effect. Roll out to a thickness of about ⅛in (3mm).

Use a needle to pierce 2 holes in the button

Cut tulip shapes from clay

8 Use the card template to cut out as many tulips as you need. Pierce 2 centre holes. Bake as for leaves.

9 **White daisies:** Roll white clay with your hand to form a long thin rope. Cut into 5 pieces each ¼in (6mm) long. Roll the pieces into small teardrop-shapes then flatten slightly to form petals.

10 Arrange the 5 petals together to form the daisy flower. Gently roll over the surface to level the petals and help to join them together.

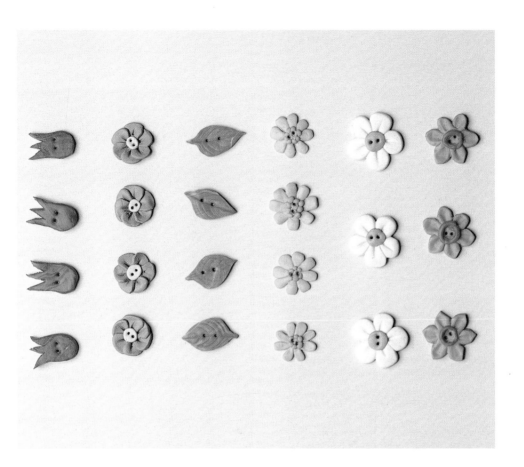

11 Mix a little yellow and orange clay together to make pale orange. Form into small balls and place one in the centre of each flower. Roll over to flatten the centre and help secure it.

12 Gently press the back of the craft knife into each petal to form a shape. Pierce 2 centre holes. Bake as for the leaves.

13 **Small yellow daisies:** Make these in a similar way to the white daisies, but with 8 small petals. Make the centres from a mixture of orange and yellow clays.

14 **Daffodils:** Mix yellow and orange clay together. Make 6 petals as for the white daisies but with slightly pointed tips. Join the petals together as for the daisies.

15 Roll out small balls of orange. Flatten into the centre of each flower. Roll a very thin rope of orange; cut into small pieces and form into circles to form the raised centres of each flower. Gently roll a cocktail stick across each petal to make it concave. Pierce 2 holes. Bake as for the leaves.

16 **Mauve and pink flowers:** Mix a little red and blue clay together with some pink to make a mauve colour. Roll out the clay thinly and make 6 petals as for the white daisies but make them slightly wider. Join the petals together by slightly overlapping the edges.

17 Mix pink and white clay together and form into small balls. Flatten into the centre of each flower. Pierce 2 centre holes. Bake as for the leaves.

Spinning in the wind

Have some fun on a windy day with a paper windmill. It's just a square of paper cut and twisted into an aerodynamic shape. When the wind blows just watch it spin!

Materials
Thin card in 2 contrasting colours
Wooden dowel, 12in (30cm) long, ½in (12mm) in diameter
Nail, 1½in (4cm) long
Wooden beads, ½in (12mm) diameter
Coloured adhesive tape

Preparation
1 From card, cut a 10in (25cm) square. Draw lines diagonally from corner to corner. Mark 1¼in (3cm) from the centre point along each line. Cut from the corners along each line up to mark.

Making the windmill
2 Using the nail, push a hole in the centre of the card. Mark and make a hole ¾in (18mm) from each corner in the middle of each right-hand section.

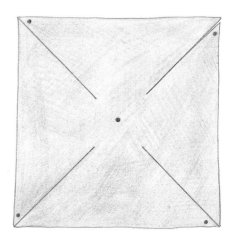

Pierce holes ¾in (18mm) from the corner in the right hand sections

3 Using pinking shears, cut a 2in (5cm)-diameter circle from contrast card. Make a hole in the centre of the circle.

4 Thread the nail through 1 bead, then through the card circle, then through the hole in each section of the windmill in turn, bending the sails to the middle. Then push the nail through the centre hole in the card, through the second bead and hammer the nail into the dowel, 1in (2.5cm) from one end.

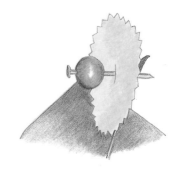

5 Decorate the wooden stick with strips of coloured adhesive tape.

Thread the nail first through the bead, then the card circle, then through the corner hole

Box of flowers

Press a selection of simple garden flowers and then use them to decorate a plain whitewood box. Once the arrangement has been sealed with varnish it will last for years.

Materials
Small whitewood trinket box
Flowers for pressing
White blotting paper (or kitchen paper)
Clear adhesive
Spray varnish
Giftwrap paper (optional)

Preparation
1 Cut the flower heads from the chosen plants in the morning after the dew has dried. Lay them between two sheets of white blotting paper (or pieces of soft kitchen paper). Place the blotting paper sheets under a pile of heavy books and leave for 4–5 weeks. (Alternatively, a flower press can be used.)

When spraying varnish, stand the piece on a small support and place it inside a large cardboard box. Turn the support to spray on all sides. A cardboard box also makes a good drying place for varnished pieces and protects the surface from dust while they are drying.

Decorating the box
2 Remove the pressed flowers. Holding the flowers in tweezers, touch a dot of adhesive to the back of each flower and spread with a fingertip. Position them over the box lid in a pleasing, overlapping arrangement. Position individual flowers round the sides of the box. Leave to dry.

Hold flowers in tweezers to prevent them from becoming damaged

3 Spray the entire box with varnish, leave to dry. Spray the box 8 or 9 times, leaving the varnish to dry completely between each coat.

Lining the box
4 Use giftwrap paper to line the box and lid. Cut the box bottom and lid pieces first, adding $\frac{1}{4}$in (6mm) all round. Snip into the edges and glue the pieces in position, pressing the excess on to the sides. Next, cut the long side strips, adding $\frac{1}{4}$in (6mm) to the ends. Glue in place. Cut the short side pieces exactly to size and glue in place.

Autumn beauty

An everlasting decoration made from dried flowers and grasses. Choose flowers in colours to suit your decor and add nuts, wooden beads and small bunches of raffia, for texture.

Materials
Dried Oasis ball, 4in (10cm) diameter
Plastic flower pot to fit inside an
   earthenware pot
Decorator's filler powder
Wooden dowel, 11in (28cm) long, ½in
   (12mm) diameter
Selection of dried flowers and grasses
Walnuts
Florists' wire
Bronze-coloured spray paint
Skein of raffene
Clear adhesive
Dried moss
Large wooden beads

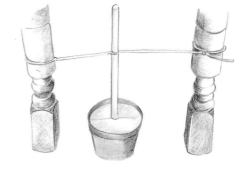

Support the wood dowel on string tied round the middle while the filler is drying

Preparation
1 Mix sufficient filler powder with water to fill the plastic pot. The mixture should be thick. Spoon into the pot and stand the dowel in the centre. Leave to dry. Spray the pot and the dowel stick bronze.

2 Spread the top of the dowel with adhesive and push on the Oasis ball.

3 Push the nuts on to a short length of florists' wire. Spray bronze.

4 Cut stems to about 4in (10cm), push flowers and grasses and the wired walnuts into the Oasis ball. Wind some raffene round your fingers. Bend a short length of wire over the centre and twist ends together. Open out the raffene. Push the wire ends into the ball. Push wooden beads on to the grass stalks.

Make wire stems on Raffene, push a wire stem into the nuts and push beads on to stalks

5 Add to the arrangement, inserting pieces of dried moss until the ball is completely covered.

6 Mask the top of the earthenware pot with a piece of paper and spray the pot bronze. Fit the plastic pot inside the earthenware pot.

Pretty pomanders

Hang aromatic dried oranges studded with cloves in the wardrobe for a natural perfume. Pomanders are traditional presents, particularly at Christmas, and their spicy scent makes them a household favourite.

Materials

Tape, ¾in (18mm) wide
Thin skinned oranges
Whole cloves
1tsp (5ml) ground cinnamon
1tsp (5ml) ground allspice
2oz (60g) orris root powder
Double-edged lace, ¾in (18mm) wide, 20in (50cm) long
Embroidered ribbon ⅜in (9mm) wide, 22in (56cm) long
Pearlized glass-headed pins

Preparation

1 Cut and pin tape to go round the orange, a second strip at right angles to the first, to quarter it. Pierce holes in the orange ¼in (6mm) apart. Push cloves into the holes to fill the quarter sections between the tapes. Remove the tapes.

2 Mix the orris root powder, allspice and cinnamon together in a plastic bag. Toss the orange in the mixture inside the bag. Remove and shake off excess powder.

3 Wrap the orange in tissue paper and leave in a dry, warm place for 2–3 weeks, to dry out.

Making the pomander

4 Cut the lace in half. Wrap each piece round the orange in the channels left by the tape. Overlap the lace ends and pin or glue to secure.

5 Beginning at the top, wrap the ribbon round the pomander placing it centrally over the lace. Pin or glue at the top and the cross-over point at the base. If the pomander is to be hung, form a loop at the top with ribbon and hold in place with glass-headed pins.

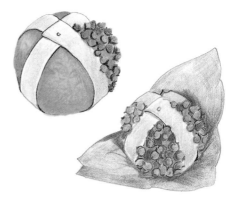

Pin tape round the orange, push cloves into the pierced holes. After tossing the orange in orris powder and spices, wrap and leave to dry

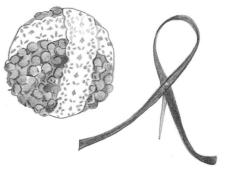

Tape lace and pin ribbons round the orange. Make a ribbon loop to pin to the top if the pomander is to be hung

All tied up

Create an unusual picture by weaving glossy embroidery cotton round bead-tipped pins. Match the thread colours to your decor for an harmonious effect.

Materials
Cork tile, 8in (20cm) square
Piece of fabric 20 × 10in (50 × 25cm)
Iron-on interfacing 20 × 10in (50 × 25cm)
64 household pins
64 blue beads
Pearl cotton in blue, pink and mauve
Curtain ring, ¾in (18mm) diameter
Adhesive

Preparation
1 Fuse the interfacing to the wrong side of the fabric. Cut the fabric in 2 pieces each 10in (25cm) square.

2 Stick the cork tile to the interfaced side of the fabric, centring it. Trim off the corners diagonally. Turn the excess fabric to the wrong side and stick in place. Place second piece of fabric right side up, over the other side of the tile, fold under the raw edges and stick in place. Slipstitch all round on the edges.

3 Sew the curtain ring to the back of the picture 1½in (4cm) from top edge and in the middle.

Using pink, work each corner from pin 1 to pin 16

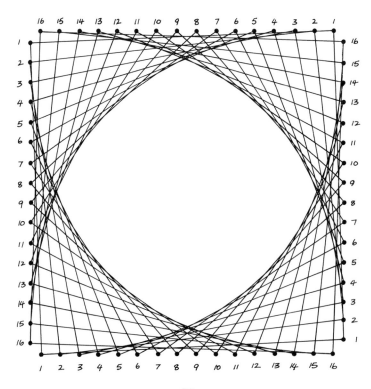

Making the picture

4 Slip 16 beads on 16 pins and hammer the pins into the tile ¾in (18mm) from the edges spacing them ⅜in (9mm) apart. Work the other 3 sides in the same way.

5 Using the blue cotton, lace round the pins from top to bottom across the tile.

6 Working first with pink cotton then with mauve, work each corner from pin 1 to pin 16, as shown in the diagram.

7 Knot the threads round the last pins. Trim ends.

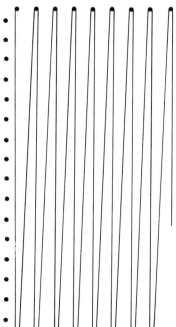

Wind blue cotton round the pins from top to bottom

Pots of style

Treat your windows to a new look with a row of smart flower pots.
Cover them with fabric to match the curtains or cushions.
Complete the look with a tartan bow.

Materials
Earthenware flower pot
PVA adhesive
Cotton print furnishing fabric
Nylon taffeta ribbon in a tartan pattern

Preparation
1 Make a small mark on the inside rim of the flower pot. Lay the pot down on a sheet of paper with mark over the paper. Holding a pencil against the rim, move the pot along the paper, until you come round to mark again. Repeat at the base of the pot. Join the two curved lines with straight lines.

2 Cut out the shape, adding $\frac{3}{8}$in (9mm) for overlap on one side edge and $\frac{3}{4}$in (18mm) on the top and base edges. Using the pattern, cut out from fabric. (Make sure that any linear pattern runs straight across, or down, the fabric.)

3 Seal the outside of the flower pot with water-diluted PVA adhesive. Leave to dry.

Spread the ribbon on paper and coat with diluted PVA adhesive

4 Coat the pot with PVA again and apply fabric all round, with the overlap even at the top and base. Overlap the side edges trimming off any excess that is required for a neat finish.

Roll the pot along the paper and pencil along the rim. Repeat at the base

Tie a bow round the flower pot while the adhesive is still wet

5 Snip into the overlaps at the top and base. Stick the overlap to the inside of the top rim. Stick the bottom overlap to the underside of the pot. Leave to dry.

6 Dilute more PVA to a thin cream consistency. Coat the ribbon. Tie the ribbon round the pot while the adhesive is still wet and tie a bow. Leave to dry. Trim the ribbon ends into 'fishtails'.

Light the way

Decorate a plain white lampshade with fabric paint designs and bring the room to life with a smart new look.

Materials

Plain white lampshade, 7in (18cm) high,
   12in (30cm)-diameter base, 4in (10cm)-
   diameter top
Water-based fabric paints
Fine-tipped paint brush
Fabric protector spray

Preparation

1 Make a paper pattern from the lampshade following the technique described for the flower pot on page 30, stage 1.

Working the design

2 Trace the pattern on pages 36–37, repeating the motifs all round the shade. The small motifs go round the upper edge. The butterflies are set at random.

3 Tape the edges of the paper pattern together and tape inside the shade, lining up the seam of the shade with the join in the paper.

Tape the traced pattern inside the shade then trace the lines on to the shade

Paint the design working towards you so that you do not smudge your work

This design would be ideal for embroidery and could be used to make curtain ties and a cushion to match the lampshade. The design could be worked entirely in satin stitch or long and short stitch, or the larger shapes could be outlined in backstitch. You might also try painting the design on the wrong side of fabric for making your own lampshade, using fabric paints, and then embroider the outlines of the flowers, leaves and butterflies on the right side. This would produce the effect of shadow embroidery.

4 Place the shade over a low-watt light bulb and trace the motifs on to the shade, using a soft pencil. Remove the pattern.

5 Mix the fabric paints and, using one colour at a time, paint the design. Work in one direction round the shade to avoid

smudging the painted areas already worked. Paint the leaves first, then the flowers and lastly the butterflies. Leave to dry completely.

6 With a soft eraser remove any pencil marks that still show on the right side of the shade. Finally spray the shade with a fabric protector.

Trace the lampshade motifs given here.
Repeat the motifs round the lampshade
pattern.

Summer baskets

Transform simple wicker baskets into decorative features to display around the home. Fill them with dried flowers, foliage, pine cones or even shiny red apples. All you need is a little fabric and some paint.

Materials
Wicker baskets with handles
Spray paint (matt or gloss)
Printed cotton fabric 36 × 20in
  (90 × 50cm)
PVA adhesive
A few fabric flowers (optional)

Preparation
1 Spray-paint the baskets.

2 Cut 2 widths of fabric each 4in (10cm) deep. Stitch into a tube, right sides facing. Press the seam open. Turn to the right side. Turn the raw edge on one end of the tube and slipstitch over the opposite end.

3 Run a gathering thread through centre of the fabric ring and pull up to fit the top of the basket. Sew in place through the wicker. Brush the fabric with diluted PVA adhesive and leave to dry.

4 Cut a piece of fabric 36 × 6in (90 × 15cm). Press in the raw edges and tie into a bow round the basket handle. Stiffen the fabric with diluted PVA. Decorate, if desired.

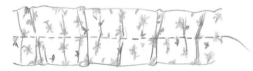

Gather the ring round the middle

Baskets for gifts
You can use the method described here to make attractive and useful baskets for bathroom accessories. If the basket is to be used for soaps it is a good idea to put a lining into the base. Stand the basket on a sheet of paper and trace round the base. Cut out for a pattern and cut the shape twice from fabric, adding ½in (12mm) all round for a seam allowance. Using the paper pattern, cut the same shape in thin wadding. Baste the wadding to the wrong side of one fabric circle, baste the second circle to the first, right sides facing. Machine-stitch all round, leaving a gap of about 4in (10cm) for turning. Turn right side out and close the gap with hemming or slipstitches. Fit the lining into the basket. If you like, you could catch the layers of the lining together with short lengths of very narrow satin ribbon, tying the ends in bows.

Stitch the 2 pieces of fabric into a tube, turn to the right side and sew one end over the other

Greetings!

Send a very special message with a hand-made card, cleverly woven with ribbons and framed in lace.

Materials
Card blanks with an oval opening
Stiff paper
¼in (6mm)-wide ribbon in colours of your
  choice
Lace edging, ⅝in (15mm) wide, 14in
  (36cm) long
Clear adhesive
Double-sided adhesive tape
Small natural sponge
Water-based paints

Making the cards
1 Mix the paint and dab over the front and back of the card, using the sponge. Leave to dry.

2 Cut a piece of paper to the same size as the card front. Place it behind the card front and pencil round the oval opening.

3 Cut ribbons to fit across the oval diagonally plus about ¼in (6mm) at each end.

4 Tape the 'warp' ribbons down first, edges touching, in a colour arrangement of your choice.

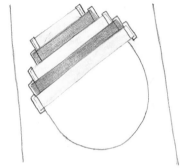

Tape down the warp ribbons first

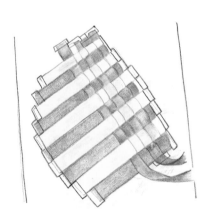

Weave ribbons through, over one, under one and tape down

Ribbon weaving would also make a very pretty St Valentine's day card. Use very narrow ribbons – ⅛ or ¼in wide (3 or 6mm) and in a range of different red colours – bright red, scarlet and crimson. Cut a heart shape from the front of a card blank. Glue the ribbon weaving behind the heart then back it with white paper. Write a loving message inside.

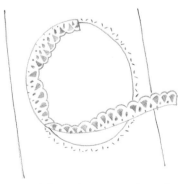

Stick lace round the oval opening in the card

5 Weave the 'weft' ribbons over and under the 'warp' ribbons, taping down at both ends.

6 Stick lace edging round the oval opening, overlapping the edges at the bottom of the oval to neaten.

7 Using double-sided tape, fix the piece of paper with the woven ribbon oval on it behind the opening in the card front, positioning it exactly in the oval opening.

8 Fold up the card.

Frame up

Frame two favourite photographs side by side in an attractive fabric-covered frame. Matched to furnishings, the frame makes a pretty bedroom accessory.

Materials

Printed cotton fabric, 15in (38cm) square
Thin mounting card, 15in (38cm) square
Iron-on lightweight interfacing, 15in (38cm) square
Fabric adhesive
Clear adhesive
Ribbon, ¼in (6mm)-wide, 4in (10cm)
Narrow braid, 25in (64cm)
2 small ribbon roses
Piece of acetate, 9 × 6in (23 × 15cm)
Piece of white paper, 9 × 6in (23 × 15cm)
Adhesive tape

Preparation

1 From card, cut a back and front 8¾ × 6in (22 × 15cm). Cut a spacing strip for the bottom edge 8¾ × ⅜in (22cm × 9mm), two strips for the sides 5⅝ × ⅜in (14.5cm × 9mm) and one strip for the centre 5⅝in × ¾in (14.5cm × 18mm).

2 Trace the oval shape and trace down twice on to one piece of card. Score round the outlines first with the tip of a craft knife, then go round again, deeper, until the card is cut through cleanly.

3 Cut one stand from card, following the measurements given.

Making the frame

4 Fuse the interfacing to the wrong side of the fabric. Place the stand piece of card on the fabric and mark round twice. Cut out both shapes adding ⅜in (9mm) all round to one of them. Stick the piece of card to the centre of the larger fabric shape. Turn in the side and bottom edges only and stick on the wrong side.

5 Stick one end of the ribbon to the back of the stand in the middle of the bottom edge. Stick the smaller piece of fabric over the back of the stand covering the ribbon.

6 Stick the spacing strips to the side, centre and bottom edge of the frame front. Place it on the interfaced fabric and mark round. Cut out adding ⅜in (9mm) all round.

Trace the oval shape and trace down twice on card

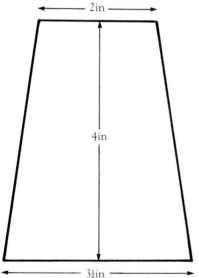

2in

4in

3⅛in

Copy this diagram on card and cut out for the stand

7 Stick the card centrally to the wrong side of the fabric. Turn the edges to the wrong side and stick in place, making neat corners. Cut out round the ovals, ⅜in (9mm) from the card edges, snip into the fabric and stick down on the wrong side.

8 Place the stand centrally on the frame back and pencil along the top edge. Cut along the pencilled line to make a slit. Cover the frame back with fabric in the same way as for the front. Cut the fabric along the slit.

9 Position the stand on the back, the bottom edges level. Pull the raw edges of fabric on the top edge of the stand through the slit to the wrong side of the back. Tape down. Stick the remaining end of ribbon to the wrong side of the back. Cut and stick a piece of white paper to wrong side of the frame back.

10 Stick the front frame to the back, spreading stick adhesive along the spacing strips only, leaving the top edge open.

11 Cut 2 pieces of acetate each 5½ × 3½in (13 × 8cm) and slot into each side of frame behind the oval openings.

12 Stick braid round the ovals bringing the ends together at the bottom of the oval. Stick a small ribbon rose over the join in the braid.

43

Ball of roses

*Create a beautiful decoration from ribbon roses pushed into a ball.
Add a hanging ribbon and perhaps ribbon streamers.*

Materials
White polystyrene ball, 4in (10cm) in
  diameter
Pastel coloured single-face satin ribbons,
  1½ (4cm), 1in (2.5cm) and ⅛in (3mm)
  wide
Stem wire and florists' wire
Florists' green stem binding tape
Silk or plastic rose leaves

Preparation
1 For the large roses cut 24in (60cm)
lengths of ribbon, for the small roses cut
14in (36cm) lengths of ribbon. Bend over
one end of a stem wire. Thread the
florists' wire into the hook and wind it
round to fasten.

Making a rose
2 Take the end of the ribbon and fold it
over the top of the wire hook, secure
with florists' wire. Pull the ribbon out to
one side and wrap it round the covered
wire 3–4 times and secure with wire.

3 To form the petals, fold the ribbon
diagonally away from the flower head,
then turn the rose centre to the middle of
the fold. Carry on turning the rose until
the ribbon is straight again. Continue
forming petals until you reach the end of
the ribbon, winding the florists' wire
round the base to hold the petals in place.

4 To complete the rose, bring the ribbon
end down to the bottom of the flower
and bind it firmly. Cut off the wire.

5 Trim the stem wire to 2in (5cm). Bind
the stem with florists' tape. Begin at the
base of the flower, sticking it firmly in
place. Gently stretching the tape, turn the
rose until the whole stem is covered.
Trim the end.

Making ribbon loops
6 Cut an 18in (45cm) length of ⅛in
(3mm)-wide ribbon. Make a hooked stem
wire as for the roses. Form the end of the
ribbon into a loop about 4½in (11.5cm)
long and bind it to the stem.

7 Make 3–4 more loops, binding each
one in place. Trim the stem and cover
with tape in the same way as for the rose.

Making the ball
8 Using a knitting needle, make a hole
through the centre of the polystyrene
ball. Bend a hook on a stem wire. Push
the other end through the ball. Trim the
wire end, bend a hook.

9 Push roses and ribbon loops into the
ball to cover it. Push leaves in between
the roses. Tie a hanging loop of 1½in
(4cm)-wide ribbon to the top hook. If
you like, knot streamers of narrow
ribbon to the bottom hook.

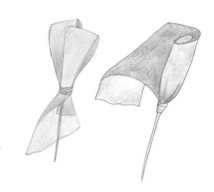

Fold and wire the ribbon over the hook on
the stem wire

44

Bind ribbon loops to cover the hook on
the stem wire

Push a long, hooked stem wire through the ball,
bend the end into a hook

45

TWO

Needlecrafts

Hanging fragrance

Bring the scents of summer into your wardrobe with these pretty fabric-covered hangers. Make lacy pot pourri sachets, to tie to the hook with satin ribbon.

Materials
Wooden coat hanger
Wadding
Floral print fabric
Net (for inside the sachet)
Cotton lawn for the sachet
Lavender or pot pourri
$\frac{5}{8}$in (15mm)-wide lace edging
1in (2.5cm)-wide double-edged lace
1in (2.5cm)-wide cut-work guipure lace
$\frac{1}{4}$in (6mm)-wide feather edge satin ribbon
$\frac{1}{2}$in (12mm)-wide satin ribbon

Preparation
1 Wrap the hanger in wadding and stitch in place.

2 Cut and make a rouleau strip (see Better Techniques) as long as the hanger hook, closing one end. Thread over the hook and sew to the wadding at the base of the hook.

Covering the hanger
3 Cut a strip of the print fabric twice the length of the hanger by 6$\frac{1}{4}$in (16cm). Press a $\frac{5}{8}$in (15mm) hem on both long edges. Fold in half with right sides together, pin and stitch ends. Turn to right side.

4 Fold the strip and mark the centre. Using a doubled thread, work a row of gathering along the folded edges. Wind the thread ends round a pin in a figure-of-eight. Work gathering along the top edge also, joining the folded edges together up to the centre.

5 Insert one end of the hanger and pull up the threads to fit. Fasten off the top threads at the hook, stitching through the rouleau covering the hook to secure.

6 Work gathering along the remaining top edge of the hanger cover in the same way. Fasten off.

Sachet
7 Cut a piece of lawn 7 × 5in (17.5 × 12.5cm). Turn double hems on the short sides. Stitch. Lay the fabric flat. Stitch lace edging over the hemmed edges. Stitch guipure lace across the middle. Stitch the double-edged lace between the middle and edges.

8 Fold the sachet right sides facing, pin and stitch the long seam. Turn right side out.

9 Make a net insert by cutting a 4$\frac{3}{4}$in (12cm) square. Fold in half and stitch the edges together. Gather up one end and fasten off. Fill with lavender or pot pourri, gather up the remaining end and fasten off.

Follow this arrangement for the lace decoration on the sachet

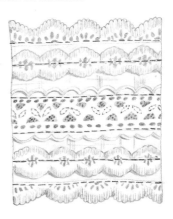

10 Place the sachet inside the outer sachet. Gather up both ends, tie with the narrow ribbon and finish with a bow. Cut a 7in (18cm)-length of narrow ribbon. Fold in half and sew the ends to the inside top of the sachet. Loop the sachet over the hanger hook.

11 Tie ½in (12mm)-wide ribbon round the hook into a bow, holding the sachet ribbon in place.

One for the pot

Bouquet garni sachets make ideal gifts for cooks. Store them in a pretty PVC holder to hang beside the cooker.

Materials
Patterned PVC, 25 × 10in (52 × 25cm)
Bias binding, 1¼yd × ½in (1.20m × 12mm)
Muslin, 30 × 12in (76 × 30cm) (makes 10)
Dried bouquet garni herbs (thyme,
   parsley, bay leaf)
Strong white thread
Curtain ring, ½in (12mm) diameter

Preparation
1 From the PVC cut two 8in (20cm) squares.

2 Cut another square for the front pocket piece, cutting one corner off diagonally.

Making the holder
3 Bind the top of the pocket with bias binding.

4 Place the 2 squares with wrong sides together with the pocket on top. Bind round the outer edge, catching in the pocket edges.

5 Hand-sew a curtain ring to the back of the top corner.

Sachets
6 From muslin, cut 6in (15cm)-diameter circles using pinking shears.

7 With strong thread, gather round the circle, 1in (2.5cm) from the outer edge. Place a small amount of dried herbs in the centre of each circle. Pull up both ends of thread together and tie. Tie threads together again, 7in (18cm) from the last knot, to form a loop. This loop will slip over the handle when the bouquet garni is in the saucepan.

Bind the top of the pocket with bias binding

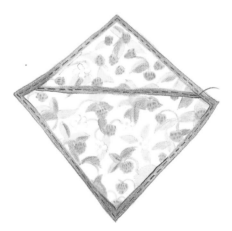

Bind round the outer edges of the squares, catching in the pocket

Working with PVC
PVC is easy to cut out and handles just like any other fabric. Some people, however, find it tricky to stitch. If the fabric sticks to the base plate, slip tissue paper between the PVC and the machine.

Memories

Decorate the covers of a plain album with silk and beads and make it extra-special for wedding memories or for baby's first pictures.

Materials
Album to cover, 11 × 9in (26 × 23cm)
Plain silk fabric, 38 × 13in (96.5 × 33cm)
Vilene Quiltex, 20 × 13in (50 × 33cm)
Gold Lurex machine thread
Matching sewing thread
Small gold beads
Pearl button

Preparation
1 Cut 2 pieces of silk, each 19⅝ × 12½in (50 × 31cm) and a piece of Vilene Quiltex the same size. Fuse the Vilene to the wrong side of one piece of silk.

2 Put the Lurex thread on the spool of the sewing machine. Following the pre-printed lines, quilt the fabric.

Making the album cover
3 Make a 5in (12.5cm) long strip of silk fabric rouleau for the fastening loop (refer to Better techniques).

4 Hand-sew a gold bead at each intersection of the quilting.

5 Cut 2 cover sleeves from silk, each 12½ × 8¼in (31 × 21cm). Turn a double ¼in (6mm)-wide hem on one long edge. Pin and stitch.

6 Baste the rouleau loop centrally on the back edge of the quilted fabric.

7 Place a sleeve to each end of the quilted fabric, right sides together and raw edges matching. Pin the second piece of silk on top. Stitch round, leaving one end open. Turn to the right side.

8 Slip the album covers into the sleeves. Sew the button to the front of the cover to correspond with the rouleau loop.

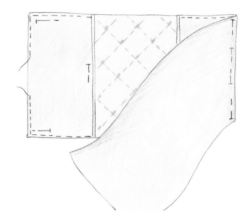

Place the sleeves in position, pin the silk fabric lining on top

Roses and pearls
For a different decoration, make a spray of cream and white ribbon roses. Using 1in (2.5cm) ribbon, fold roses as described on page 44 but catching the base of the rose together with stitches instead of using a wire stem. Fold ribbon leaves from 2in (5cm) lengths of ribbon. Sew the roses and leaves to the album cover in a pleasing arrangement. Sew 2 or 3 pearl beads to the rose centres. Sew a few more pearl beads around the arrangement. Stems can be made by catching down very narrow ribbons.

Bathing beauties

Plain towels get a bright new look with smart jacquard ribbon and pretty lace trims. They are simple to sew and the perfect complement to a stylish bathroom.

Materials
Plain towels
Easy-care jacquard woven ribbons, 1in and ⅜in (2.5cm and 9mm) wide
Doubled edged lace ⅝in (15mm) wide
Lace edging ⅜in (9mm) wide

Preparation
1 **Peach towel:** Cut 4 pieces of the lace edging to the width of the towel plus ½in (12mm). Cut a piece of the wider ribbon to the same length.

2 Baste 2 lengths of lace at each end of the towel (over the embossed area) facing outwards and ¾in (18mm) apart. Tuck under ¼in (6mm) at each end to neaten.

Working the design
3 Baste the ribbon between the lace edgings, neatening the ends as before.

4 Machine-stitch down the edges of the ribbon catching in the lace edging on either side as you stitch. Make sure you stitch in the same direction on both edges to prevent puckering.

5 Decorate both ends of the towel in the same way.

6 **Blue towel:** Cut 2 pieces of double-edged lace to the width of the towel plus ½in (12mm). Place one piece at each end of the towel over the embossed area, tucking under ¼in (6mm) at each end to neaten. Pin, baste and stitch, down the middle of the lace.

7 Cut 4 pieces of the narrow jacquard ribbon to the towel width plus ½in (12mm). Position a ribbon either side of the lace, tucking them under the lace edges. Tuck the ends under to neaten. Pin, baste and stitch in place down both edges of the ribbons.

8 Work both ends of the towel in the same way.

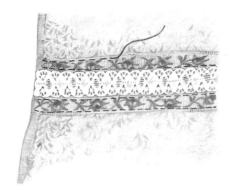

Position the ribbons either side of the lace

Stitch the ribbon between the strips of lace

Window style

Honeycomb curtain heading tape is ideal for making smart tie-backs. Either make them in the same fabric as the curtains or choose a patterned fabric to tone with a plain fabric. They are so simple they could be made in an evening.

Materials
Furnishing fabric, 48 × 15½in (120 × 39cm)
Smocked honeycomb-style curtain
   heading tape, 3yd (2.8m) long
Curtain rings, ½in (12mm) diameter

Preparation
1 Cut 2 strips of fabric each 48 × 7¾in (120 × 19.5cm). Turn in 1½in (4cm) on both long edges and press. Turn in 1in (2.5cm) at each short end, mitring the corners.

Making the tie-backs
2 Cut 2 pieces of heading tape to the same length as the fabric strips, plus 2in (5cm). Knot the cords at one end.

3 Turn under the tape ends, 1in (2.5cm). Pin, and baste to the wrong side of the fabric, centring the tape.

4 Machine-stitch 4 rows across the tape and then down the short ends.

5 Pull up the cords until a smocked effect is formed. Tie the cords together, wind up the ends.

6 Sew a curtain ring to each end of the tie-backs. These can hold the wound-up cords at the same time.

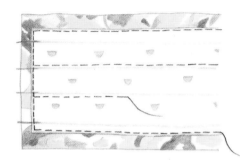

Work 4 rows of machine-stitching across the tape, then stitch down the short sides

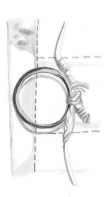

Wind up the cords, push through the rings to hold them securely in place

Guard that door

Sew a smiling crocodile to guard your door against draughts. He can follow you around the house to keep each room warm and cosy.

Materials

Printed cotton fabric, 40 × 18in
(102 × 45cm)
Wide green ricrac braid, 28in (70cm)
Washable polyester toy filling

Narrow green ricrac braid, 30in (76cm)
12in (30cm) squares of felt, emerald
green, yellow; scraps of dark green,
pink
Pair of joggle eyes, ¾in (18mm) diameter

Preparation

1 On squared paper draw the shapes for the main body and the flower from the graph pattern on pages 60–61.

2 Using the paper pattern, cut 2 body pieces from printed fabric. Cut 4 green and 4 yellow felt feet. Cut the emerald green inner eyes and dark green outer eyes from felt using pinking shears. Cut the flower petals from pink felt with the inner flower in yellow felt. Cut a small green felt circle for the flower centre.

Making the crocodile

3 Pin the wide ricrac braid to the right side along the top edges of one body piece. Place the bodies with right sides together. Pin, baste and stitch, all round catching in the braid and leaving an opening along the base edge. Turn the body to the right side. Fill the crocodile firmly. Turn in the opening edges and slipstitch together to close.

Cut 'v's into one edge of the yellow felt strips

4 Stick the joggle eyes to the inner, green eyes, then stick to the outer, dark green eyes. Stick the completed eyes either side of head.

Draw the graph pattern on squared paper (scale 1 sq = 1in (2.5cm)

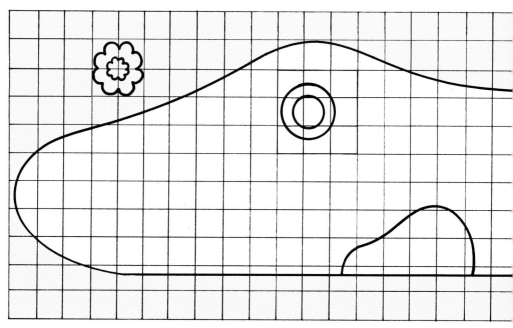

5 For the mouth, cut 2 strips of yellow felt 15 × 1in (38 × 2.5cm). Cut one edge of each piece into 'Vs'. Stick to the head round the mouth with the points facing inwards for teeth. Stick the narrow, green ricrac braid round the upper edge of the felt mouth.

6 Make up the flower, stick to one side of the mouth.

7 Stitch the feet together in pairs of green and yellow. Fill slightly. Sew the legs to either side of the body.

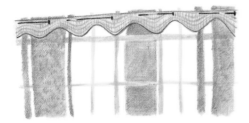

Pin the ricrac braid along the top edge of the body piece

Crocodile toy

You can use the basic crocodile pattern to make a long toy for a small child. Children find these fun to play with and drape them around their necks – or curl them into a 'nest' for a quick nap. Scraps of cotton fabric can be used. Cut 14in (35cm) squares of contrasting fabrics. Seam together to make a strip about 36in (90cm) long. Join the long side to make a tube. Cut 2 crocodile heads from fabric, join (inserting ricrac braid), then sew the head to the tube. Sew on eyes and mouth. Stuff the crocodile from the tail end, keeping the stuffing soft and flexible. Trim the end to a narrow tail, turn in the edges and slipstitch to close, pushing in a little more stuffing. Add felt feet if desired.

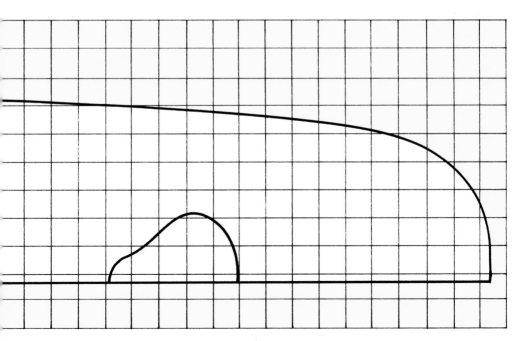

Roll up, roll up!

Breakfast rolls keep warm in this pretty pocketed basket lining. Match the lining to your tablecloth and napkins for a co-ordinated effect. It can also be used to display fruit, such as oranges, peaches, apricots, pears or apples.

Materials
Printed cotton fabric, 36 × 12in
    (90 × 30cm)
Gingham check fabric, 36 × 12in
    (90 × 30cm)
Ricrac braid ½in (12mm) wide, 3yd (2.7m)
    long
2 press fasteners
12in (30cm)-diameter basket

Preparation
1 From each of the fabrics cut out 3 circles each 12in (30cm) in diameter (6 circles in total).

2 Pin and baste ricrac braid round 3 circles of the same fabric ½in (12mm) from the edge. Place the circles together in pairs, one print to one gingham, wrong sides facing.

3 Pin, baste and stitch all round, leaving an opening. Trim the seam allowance and turn right side out. Turn in the opening edges and slipstitch to close.

Stitch the third circle in place, between each segment to within 3in (7.5cm) of the centre

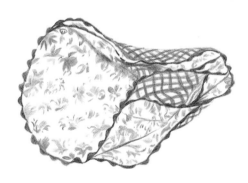

Press fasteners form the pockets when fastened

Stitch the 2 circles together dividing them into 6 segments

Try making the basket lining from spotted voile or lawn, trimming the edges with narrow cotton lace. Interline the circles with white cotton.

4 Place 2 circles together, gingham to gingham, pin and topstitch together stitching across the circles from side to side dividing the circle into 6 segments.

5 Add the third circle on top. Pin and stitch to the middle circle between each

segment, to within 3in (7.5cm) of the centre.

6 Stitch the press fasteners to the top circle in adjoining segments. Fasten together across the circle, to create the pockets. Place the lining in the basket.

Table talk

Make tea time extra special with an appliqué tablecloth and matching napkins.

Materials
Floral fabric, 36 × 48in (90 × 1.20m)
Plain glazed cotton fabric, $2\frac{1}{4}$yd × 48in
   (2 × 1.20m)
Bondaweb

Preparation
1 Roughly cut the floral motifs from the fabric. Fuse Bondaweb to the wrong side of each piece. Cut out the motifs closely.

Making the tablecloth
2 Cut a 48in (1.20m) square from the plain fabric. Turn a double $\frac{1}{4}$in (6mm) hem all round, mitring the corners. Pin, baste and stitch the hem.

3 Peel off the backing and position a large floral motif in each corner. Fuse in place. Add smaller motifs in between the corner motifs. Baste each in place.

4 Set your sewing machine to a close satin stitch and work round each motif.

Work machine satin stitch round the motifs

Making the napkins
5 Cut six 16in (40cm) squares from the plain fabric and turn a double $\frac{1}{4}$in (6mm)-wide hem all round, mitring the corners. Pin, baste and stitch the hem.

6 Position a single floral motif in one corner of each napkin and fuse in place. Work satin stitch all round the motif.

Fuse a large motif to each corner of the tablecloth

Lace appliqué
Scraps of washable lace can be used to decorate a plain, linen or cotton tablecloth. To appliqué, machine-stitch round a motif, using a medium-width satin stitch. Cut out and then sew the motifs to the cloth. To insert lace motifs and strips, baste the lace to the right side of the cloth, then zigzag machine-stitch all round the edges. On the wrong side, trim away the fabric, turn narrow hems and sew to neaten.

Good companions

Stitch a matching shower hat and a sponge bag to hold potions and lotions. These make ideal gifts for friends of all ages.

Materials

Printed cotton fabric, 1⅛yd (1m) × 36in (90cm)

Nylon fabric, 1⅛yd (1m) × 36in (90cm)

Pre-gathered lace edging, ¾in (18mm) wide, 3½yd (3.20m) long

Elastic, ¼in (6mm) wide, 24in (60cm) long

8in (20cm) square of heavyweight iron-on interfacing

Ribbon, ¼in (6mm) wide, 2yd (1.80m) long

Preparation

1 Shower hat: Cut a 24in (60cm)-diameter circle from both the printed fabric and nylon fabric.

Making the hat

2 Pin and stitch the lace edging to right side of the fabric circle, ⅝in (15mm) from the edge. Join the lace ends to fit the circle.

3 Place the nylon circle to the right sides of the fabric circle. Pin and stitch all round, following the previous stitching line and leaving an opening for turning. Trim the seam allowance and turn to the right side. Turn in the opening edges and slipstitch together.

4 Casing: Stitch all round the hat 1½in (4cm) from the outer edge. Stitch round again ⅜in (9mm) inside the first row of stitching.

5 Cut a small slit in the casing on the nylon side. Oversew the raw edges to neaten. Measure round the head with a piece of elastic, allowing an extra ⅜in (9mm) for overlap. Fasten a safety pin to one end of the elastic and thread through the casing. Overlap the ends and oversew together. Push the join inside the casing.

6 Sponge bag: For the sides, cut 2 pieces of fabric and 2 pieces of nylon each measuring 18 × 14in (46 × 36cm). Cut a 6in (15cm)-diameter circle from both fabric and nylon for the base. For the inside pockets, cut 2 pieces each from fabric and nylon each measuring 18 × 7in (46 × 18cm).

7 Place the fabric and nylon pocket pieces together with right sides facing. Pin and stitch the top edges. Turn right side out. Topstitch ⅜in (9mm) from the top edge.

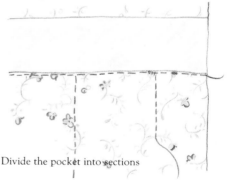

Divide the pocket into sections

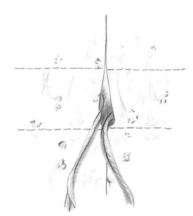

Each ribbon goes in and comes out of the same opening

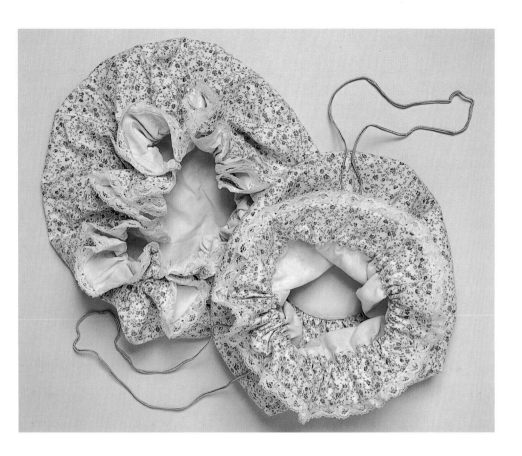

8 Place the pockets to the nylon side pieces, matching lower edges. Pin and baste together. Place the nylon side pieces right sides together. Pin and stitch the side edges. Topstitch from the pocket top to the base edges to divide each side into 3 separate pockets.

9 Place the fabric sides together with right sides facing. Pin and stitch the sides, leaving a $\frac{5}{8}$in (15mm) opening in each side about $2\frac{3}{4}$in (7cm) from the top edge. Pin and stitch lace edging to the right side all round the top edge, joining the ends together.

10 Place the nylon lining to the fabric, right sides together. Pin and stitch round the top, following the previous stitching line. Turn to the right side. Pin and baste the bottom edges together. Topstitch round the top to form a casing.

11 Fuse the interfacing to the wrong side of the fabric base. Work a row of gathering round the bottom edges of the sides. Pull up evenly to fit the fabric base. Pin and stitch. Turn under the raw edges on the nylon base and place over fabric base, wrong sides together. Pin and topstitch all round.

12 Cut the ribbon into 2 equal lengths. Thread the first length of ribbon through the casing, going in and coming out through the same opening. Knot the ends together, push the knot into the casing. Thread the second ribbon length through the casing, going and coming out through the second opening. Knot the ends and push the knot into the casing. Pull the ribbons up from each side of the bag.

Great outdoors

Nothing beats eating out-of-doors on summer days, and with these handy picnic roll-mats you can travel – and eat – in style.

Materials
(For two roll-mats)
Checked cotton fabric, 18 × 36in
  (46 × 90cm)
Spotted green cotton fabric 24 × 36in
  (60 × 90cm)
Plain yellow cotton fabric, 26 × 12in
  (65 × 30cm)
Lightweight polyester wadding 36 × 12in
  (90 × 30cm)
Heavyweight iron-on interfacing,
  36 × 12in (90 × 30cm)
Elastic, ¾in (18mm) wide, 12in (30cm)
  long

Preparation
1 From checked fabric, cut 1 piece
18 × 12in (46 × 30cm) for the back and 1
piece 8½ × 12in (21 × 30cm) for the inside
centre.

2 From plain yellow fabric, cut out 2
pieces each 6¼ × 12in (16 × 30cm) for the
inside pieces.

Making the roll-up
3 Cut a piece of interfacing the same size
as the back and fuse to the wrong side of
the checked fabric.

4 Strap holders: Cut 2 strips of checked
fabric each 7 × 2½in (17.5 × 6cm). Fold
each in half lengthways right sides facing.
Stitch on the long edges taking a ¼in
(6mm) seam. Turn right side out, press.

5 Cut the elastic in half. Thread one
piece of the elastic through the strap, pin
the ends. Make up the second strap in
the same way.

6 Pin one end of each strap to the middle of the yellow side pieces. Turn under the long edges of the checked centre piece, press and overlap the yellow pieces at each side. Pin, baste and topstitch in place, catching in the end of the strap.

7 Cut a piece of wadding the same size as the inside of the roll and pin and baste to the wrong side. Quilt the checked area of the inside only. Follow the lines of the checked fabric to make quilting easier. Use matching thread.

8 Divide the strap on one side into 3 sections by stitching across it. Pin the strap ends centrally to the outside edges of the inside.

9 Ties: Cut a piece of the spotted fabric 28 × 1½in (71 × 4cm). Fold in half lengthways right sides facing and stitch across the ends and down the length, leaving an opening centrally in the long side. Trim the seam allowance and turn through to the right side. Slipstitch the opening to close. Press. Fold the tie in half and baste in the middle of the left-hand side of the back piece.

10 Pin and baste the inside to the back, wrong sides facing. Using a piece of chalk and a cup as a guide, round off the corners. Stitch the back and inside together working close to the edge all round, catching in the straps and ties.

11 Cut 2in (5cm)-wide strips on the bias from the green spotted fabric. Join pieces until you have sufficient to go all round the roll.

12 Finish all round the roll with bias binding.

13 Napkin: Cut a 12in (30cm) square of spotted green fabric. Turn and press a double ¼in (6mm)-wide hem on the sides. Stitch. Fold the napkin and slip under the strap. Roll up and use the ties to close the roll.

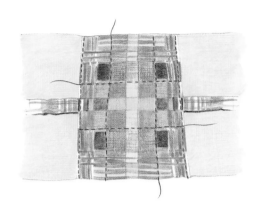

Quilt the checked area of fabric only

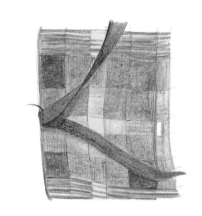

Baste the tie to the middle of the left hand side

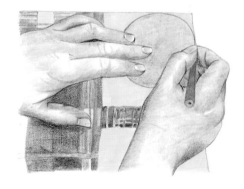

Round off the corners using a cup or glass

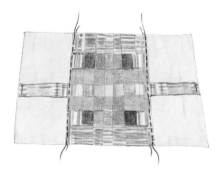

Pin the straps to the middle, topstitch the neatened checked fabric on top

72

Rosettes and bows

Soft bows and rosettes on fabric streamers are a stylish way to display pictures and prints. Match the fabric to your other soft furnishings.

ROSETTES
Materials
(For 2 rosettes on streamers)
Furnishing fabric, 36 × 40in (90 × 102cm)
2 self-covering buttons, ¾in (18mm) diameter
2 curtain rings, ½in (12mm) diameter

Preparation
1 From the fabric cut 1 strip 36 × 7½in (90 × 18cm) and 1 strip 20½ × 4½in (51 × 11cm).

Making the rosette
2 Stitch the longer strip into a ring by joining the short ends. Fold in half lengthways, raw edges together. Gather up the raw edges by hand and pull tight, forming a rosette. Fasten off the thread ends. Work the second strip in the same way.

3 Place the smaller rosette centrally on top of the larger and hand-sew together.

4 Cover the button with fabric. Sew to the centre of the rosette.

Making the streamer
5 Cut a strip of fabric 36 × 8in (90 × 20cm). Fold in half lengthways right sides facing. Cut across one end diagonally. Stitch along the diagonal end and the long edges, leaving the short, straight end open. Trim seam allowances and turn to the right side.

6 Press with the seam to one edge. Turn in the open end and hand-sew to the back of rosette.

7 Sew a curtain ring to the back of the rosette. The picture is hung just under the rosette and over the streamer.

BOW
Materials
(For 2 bows on streamers)
Furnishing fabric, 72 × 36in (180 × 90cm)
2 curtain rings, ½in (12mm) diameter

Preparation
1 From the fabric, cut a strip 10 × 23in (25 × 58cm).

Making the bow
2 Fold in half lengthways right sides facing and stitch the edges together leaving an opening centrally in the long side. Trim the seam allowances and turn to the right side. Close the open seam with slipstiches.

3 Cut the centre band 5½ × 4¾in (14 × 12cm). Fold in half lengthways, stitch the long edges. Trim the seam allowances and turn to the right side.

4 Form the bow, pleating the centre. Cover with the centre band and hand-sew at the back of the bow. Make the streamers in the same way as for the rosette streamer (stages 5 and 6). Sew the bows to the streamers and add a curtain ring at the back for hanging.

Cover the button with fabric

Hand-sew the two rosettes together

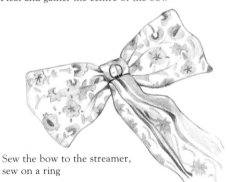

Pleat and gather the centre of the bow

Sew the bow to the streamer,
sew on a ring

Overnight guest

The perfect gift for the traveller – a comfortable pair of slip-ons in their own drawstring bag. Almost flat, the bag and slip-ons are easy to pack and take up hardly any space.

Materials
Floral fabric, 30 × 18in (75 × 46cm)
Thick card, 12 × 10in (30 × 25cm)
Craft-weight interfacing, 12 × 10in
  (30 × 25cm)
Bias binding, ½in (12mm) wide, 2¼yd
  (2.10m) long
Lace edging, ¾in (18mm) wide, 1yd (90cm)
Cord, 1 yd (90cm)

Preparation
1 Draw round a foot on a piece of stiff card. Repeat for the other foot. Cut out the 2 shapes.

Cut the strap diagonally to match the sole

2 Using the card shapes as templates cut 2 shapes from interfacing and 2 from fabric for each slip-on adding ¼in (6mm) all round to each shape.

Making the slip-ons
(Make two in the same way)
3 Sandwich the card between the 2 pieces of interfacing then between the 2 pieces of fabric. Baste, then stitch all round to hold the layers together.

4 For the cross-over straps, cut 2 pieces of fabric each 16 × 2in (40 × 5cm). Press the strips in half lengthways. Baste lace along the raw edges, bind to neaten with bias binding.

Bind round the sole, catching in the straps

5 Place the foot on the sole and place the straps over the foot in a cross, to fit. Pin together. Cut the strap ends diagonally to match the sole. Pin. Bind round the outer edges of the sole, catching in the strap ends.

Making the bag
6 For the bag cut a piece of fabric

measuring 14 × 13½in (36 × 34cm). Fold in half right sides facing. Pin and stitch across the base and up the side edges, leaving a ⅜in (9mm) opening 1in (2.5cm) from the top edge.

7 Turn a ¼in (6mm) hem then a ¾in (18mm) hem to form a casing. Pin and stitch all round, just above the fold of the ¼in (6mm) hem. Thread the cord through the casing, knot the ends.

8 Tuck the slip-ons into the bag.

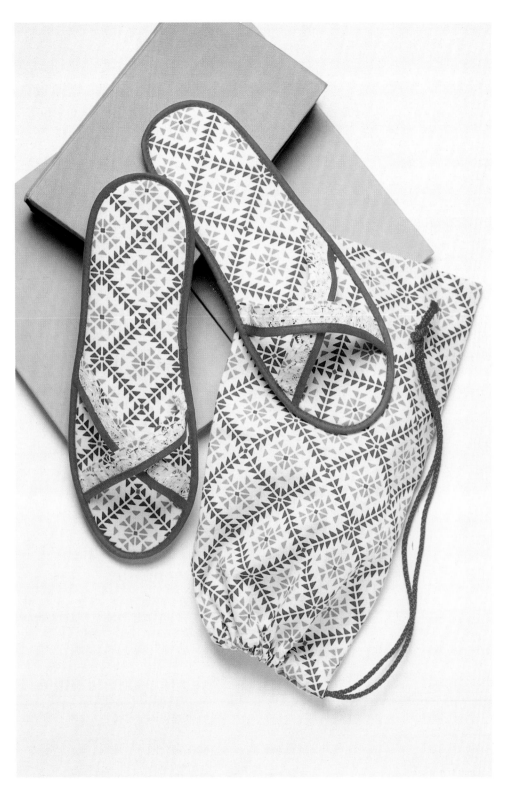

Sew easy

Sewing baskets make a wonderful gift for both young and older needleworkers. Inside this dolly-bag basket there is a pin cushion and needlecase. If you are making it for a gift, why not add a pair of scissors and a tape measure?

Materials

Basket, 5in (13cm) high, 9in (23cm) in diameter at the top, 7in (18cm) in diameter at the base
Printed cotton fabric 36in (90cm) square
Ribbon, ¼in (6mm) wide, 2yd (1.80cm)
Shirring elastic, 30in (75cm)
Elastic, 1½yd (1.40cm)
Heavyweight interfacing, 10in (25cm) square
Washable polyester toy filling
Dark blue felt, 12in (30cm) square
5 small ribbon roses
Soft embroidery cotton

BASKET

1 Cut 2 pieces of fabric each 15¼ × 7¼in (38 × 16cm) for the basket's lining. Cut 1 piece for the pockets, 36 × 5in (90 × 12.5cm). For the basket base, cut 2 circles to the size of the base plus ⅜in (15mm) all round. Cut 1 base circle from the interfacing.

2 For the basket cover, cut 2 pieces of fabric each 18 × 10½in (45 × 26cm).

3 Pockets: Stitch a ¼in (6mm) hem along the top long edge. Insert shirring elastic, secure at each end. Do not draw up.

4 Measure and mark the strip into 6 equal sections for 6 pockets. Measure and mark one of the lining pieces in the same way. Matching the bottom edges, stitch the pocket piece to the lining down the marked lines.

5 Fold the lining in half, right sides facing, and stitch the short edges together, catching in the ends of elastic.

6 Stitch the short sides of the second lining piece, right sides facing.

7 Baste the 2 lining pieces together, right sides facing, round the top edge. Turn right side out. Press. Topstitch round, ⅜in (9mm) from the edge for a casing.

8 Gather up the bottom edges together.

9 Sandwich the interfacing between the two base circles. Baste together. Turn the lining inside out. Baste the lining to the basket base, adjusting the gathers to fit.

10 Stitch the lining to the base. Neaten the raw edges with zig-zag machine-stitching. Turn the completed basket lining right side out.

11 Basket cover: Stitch the 2 pieces of fabric together on the short ends, right sides facing. Press seams open. Turn to right side.

12 Fold the ring of fabric double, almost in half, so that ⅜in (9mm) hangs longer at the outside (this is for hem neatening later).

13 Pin, baste and stitch a ⅜in (9mm)-wide casing round the top, 1in (2.5cm) down from the top edge.

14 Now turn the extra ⅜in (9mm) over to make a narrow double hem round the bottom edges. Make a casing, as you did for the top edge.

15 Unpick a few stitches of the side seams over the top casing. Cut the ribbon in half. Thread the ribbons through the casing. Overlap and sew the ends.

16 Unpick a few stitches on the inside of the bottom casing. Cut a 26in (66cm) length of elastic, thread through the casing. Overlap the ends, sew to join, sew up casing.

Stitch the pocket piece down the marked lines

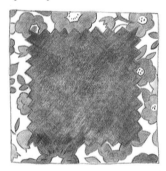

Topstitch the felt to the top fabric piece

Make an embroidery thread loop fastening on the back edge of the case

PIN CUSHION

17 Cut 2 pieces of fabric 6in (15cm) square. Cut a piece of felt, with pinking shears, 3in (7.5cm) square.

18 Topstitch the felt to the right side of one fabric piece.

19 Stitch the fabric squares together, right sides facing, leaving an opening in one side. Turn right side out, fill firmly. Close the opening with slipstitches. Decorate with 2 small ribbon roses.

NEEDLECASE

20 Cut 2 pieces of fabric each 10×6in (25×15cm). Cut a piece of heavyweight interfacing to the same size. Baste the interfacing to the wrong side of one fabric piece. Place the fabric pieces together with right sides facing. Stitch all round leaving an opening in one side. Trim seam allowances. Turn to the right side. Close the opening with slipstitches. Press.

21 Using pinking shears, cut 2 pieces of felt $7\frac{1}{2} \times 3\frac{1}{2}$in ($19 \times 9$cm). Centre them on the open needlecase. Using embroidery cotton, take a large stitch through the centre from the outside and tie the ends together in a bow on the spine.

22 Sew a small loop of embroidery cotton to the back of the case for a fastening. Sew a ribbon rose to the top. Sew another rose to the front as a button.

Cuddle and squeak

Your baby will enjoy mealtimes all the more with this happy bear bib, because the bear squeaks when its nose is pressed.

Materials

Towelling facecloth, 12in (30cm) square
Striped cotton fabric, 20 × 14in
  (50 × 36cm)
A flat squeaker
White bias binding, ½in (12mm) wide, 2yd
  (1.90m)
Oddment of towelling in a contrast
  colour
Black colour-fast cotton fabric, for
  features

Preparation

1 From the graph pattern, draw the bib
pattern on squared paper (scale 1 sq = 1in
(2.5cm). Trace the bear's face and ears.

2 Cut the bib shape twice, on the fold,
from the striped fabric. Cut the bear's
face and outer ears from the towelling
facecloth. Cut the inner ears from the
towelling oddments. Cut the nose and 2
eyes from the black fabric.

Making up the bib

3 Baste the bear face, the outer ears and
the inner ears on to one bib piece. Pin
and baste. Work machine satin stitch
round inner and outer ears and then
round the face.

4 Pin and baste the eyes and nose on the
face. Work machine satin stitch all
round, adding a curved mouth under the
nose.

5 Place the bibs together and mark the
position of the squeaker behind the nose
on the back bib piece. Cut a 3in (7.5cm)
square of striped fabric and stitch to the
back bib to contain the squeaker, leaving
one side open. Insert the squeaker and
complete the stitching.

6 Baste the bibs together with the
squeaker in between. Stitch all round.
Bind round all the outer edges with bias
binding, stitching with zig-zag stitches.

7 Bind round the neck edge in the same
way, but leave 9½in (24cm) lengths of
binding on each side for ties. Continue
the stitching up the ties, tucking in the
raw ends to neaten.

Graph pattern for the bib. Scale 1 sq = 1in (2.5cm)

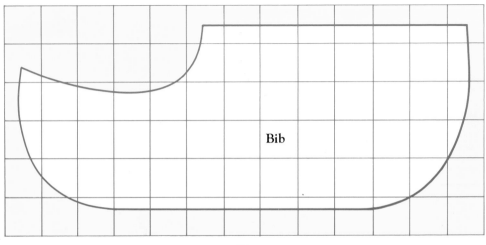

Bib

84

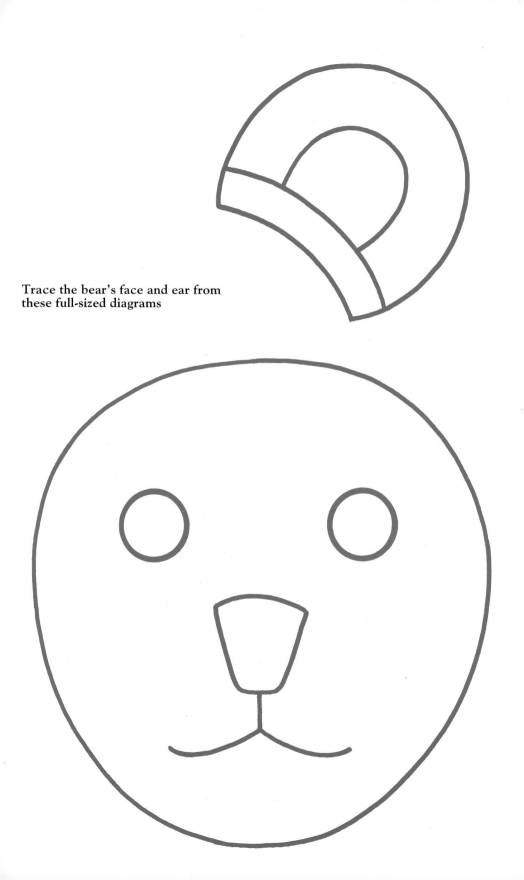

Trace the bear's face and ear from these full-sized diagrams

Pretty and practical

Add a touch of glamour to your dressing table with quilted accessories. Display your brooch collection on a neat cushion, conceal a tissue box under a smart cover and make a fabric tray to hold all your bits and pieces.

Materials
Cotton print fabric, 35 × 20in (89 × 50cm)
Pre-gathered lace edging, ⅝in (15mm)
  wide, 4yd (3.70m)
Vilene Quiltex, 30 × 16in (75 × 40cm)
Blue ribbon, ¼in (6mm) wide, 1yd (90cm)
Thin card, 12 × 6in (30 × 15cm)
Small amount of polyester toy filling
Old tissue box, for a pattern

BROOCH CUSHION
Preparation
1 From the print fabric cut 2 pieces, each
7¾ × 5¾in (19 × 14.5cm). Cut 2 pieces the
same size from the Quiltex. Fuse the
Quiltex to the wrong side of the fabric
pieces. Quilt both pieces following the
quilting lines.

Making the brooch cushion
2 Mark a rectangle 1¼in (3cm) in from
the edges on one quilted piece; this will
be the front. Baste and stitch lace round
the front, ⅝in (15mm) from the edges,
joining the ends together. Pin and
topstitch lace round the marked
rectangle, joining the ends together.

3 Place the second quilted piece to the
front, right sides facing. Pin and stitch all
round, following the previous stitching
line and leaving an opening on one side.
Trim the seam allowances and across the
corners. Turn right side out. Stuff firmly.
Turn in the opening edges and slipstitch
together.

4 Tie a small blue ribbon bow and sew
to one corner.

TRAY
Preparation
5 Cut 2 pieces of fabric each measuring
11½ × 10in (29 × 25cm). Cut 2 pieces of
Quiltex to match. Fuse the Quiltex to the
wrong side of the fabric pieces. Quilt in
the same way as for brooch cushion.

Making the tray
6 Pin and stitch lace to the right side of
one quilted piece, ⅝in (15mm) from the
edges joining the ends together to fit.
Place the quilted pieces together with
right sides facing. Stitch all round,
following previous stitching line, and
leaving one short side open. Trim corners
and seam allowances. Turn right side out.

The instructions for the tray could
be adapted to make a larger tray
divided into 4 sections. Cut the
fabrics both longer and wider and cut
the card stiffeners to about 2in (5cm)
wide for deeper sides. Cut 2 pieces of
thin card to half the width of the tray
by the depth and 2 pieces to half the
length of the tray by the depth.
Cover the cards with medium-weight
interfacing. For each piece of card
cut a piece of fabric to the actual size
and another piece ¼in (6mm) larger all
round. Baste the smaller piece of
fabric to the card, matching edges,
then apply the larger piece to the
other side, turning in the edges and
hemming all round. Catch the
dividers to the inside tray and in the
middle.

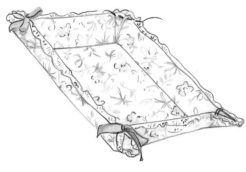

Slip the stiffeners in and pin against the seams

Hold the tray sides together with 2 or 3 stitches at the corners

7 From card, cut 2 pieces $5\frac{1}{2} \times 1\frac{1}{2}$in ($14 \times 4$cm) for stiffening the short sides, 2 pieces $7 \times 1\frac{1}{2}$in (18×4cm) for the long sides and 1 piece $7 \times 5\frac{1}{2}$in (18×14cm) for the base.

8 Slide one short side stiffener inside the fabric and pin centrally against the opposite seam. Slide in both long side stiffeners and pin centrally against the long sides. Slide in the base stiffener and pin to hold in position, 3mm ($\frac{1}{8}$in) from the side stiffeners. Stitch round the base in the $\frac{1}{8}$in (3mm) gap, to hold the stiffeners in place. Finally slide in the remaining side stiffeners. Turn in open side seam allowance and slipstitch.

9 Fold up the tray sides and hold together with 2 or 3 stitches at each corner. Tie small blue ribbon bows. Sew a bow to each corner.

TISSUE BOX COVER
Preparation
10 Cut a piece of fabric 16in (40cm) square. Cut a piece of Quiltex to match and fuse to the wrong side of the fabric. Quilt, as before.

11 Use the old tissue box as a pattern. Cut away the bottom. Cut up the sides to the top. Spread the box flat. Pencil round the outline of the box and the oval

opening. Remove the box pattern and mark a $\frac{5}{8}$in (15mm) seam allowance all round the outer edge. Cut out.

Making the cover
12 Cut out the oval hole, cutting $\frac{1}{2}$in (12mm) within the pencilled oval. Pin and baste lace round the pencilled oval, joining the ends together to fit. Cut a 1in (2.5cm)-wide strip of fabric on the bias, long enough to go round the opening. Bind round the oval.

13 Match the side edges, right sides facing. Stitch. Neaten and press the seams open. Turn a double $\frac{1}{4}$in (6mm) hem all round the bottom edge. Stitch. Pin and topstitch 2 rows of lace round the bottom edge of the cover, so that they overlap. Join the lace ends to fit.

14 Tie a small blue ribbon bow and sew to one side of the opening.

Interfacing fabrics
The Quiltex material not only helps you to quilt fabric but also gives it a firmer feel which is ideal for making tissue box covers and trays. If you prefer not to quilt the fabric, use heavy-weight non-woven interfacing to back the fabric, basting it to the wrong side before making up the item.

Kitchen capers

Make a collection of smart and practical accessories for the kitchen, mixing and matching florals and stripes.

Materials
Striped fabric, 1¾yd × 54in (1.60 × 137cm)
Floral fabric, 18 × 36in (46 × 90cm)
Medium-weight washable polyester
  wadding, 36 × 20in (90 × 50cm)
Curtain interlining, 33 × 6in (84 × 15cm)

TEA COSY
Preparation
1 On squared paper, draw a pattern from the graph pattern. Cut 4 shapes from striped fabric (2 for the lining) and 2 pieces from wadding.

Making the cosy

2 Place a piece of wadding to the wrong side of a main fabric piece, place the lining on top. Stitch the lower edge. Turn the lining to the inside. Work both sides of the cosy in the same way.

3 Make up a 2½in (6cm) length of rouleau in floral fabric for loop (see Better techniques) and place one end at the centre top of one cosy piece. Place cosy pieces together with wrong sides facing. Stitch round the curved edges.

4 From the floral fabric, cut a 1½in (4cm)-wide bias strip for binding the teacosy. Apply the bias binding catching in the other end of the loop.

EGG COSIES

Preparation

5 Draw the shape from the graph pattern, then cut 4 pieces of fabric, 2 from the floral for the main cosy, 2 from striped lining. Cut 2 pieces from wadding.

Making the cosies

6 Place the main cosy and lining pieces together, wrong sides facing, with the wadding in between. Cut bias strips from the striped fabric and bind the bottom edges as before.

7 Place 2 cosy pieces together and make up a 2in (5cm) length of striped rouleau for the top loop. Baste to the top of the cosy and bind the edges (as for tea cosy) using striped fabric bias strips.

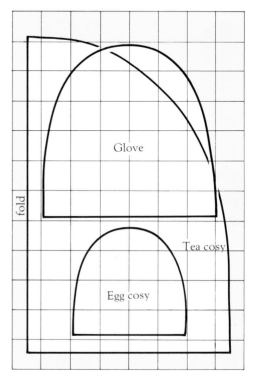

Draw the patterns for the teacosy, egg cosy and oven glove on squared paper (scale 1 sq = 1in (2.5cm)

APRON

Preparation

8 On tracing paper, draw the half apron pattern. Fold the striped fabric in half and place the pattern to the fold. Cut out.

9 For the neck strap, cut a piece of floral fabric 20 × 1¾in (50 × 4.5cm). Fold in half lengthways wrong sides facing. Stitch the long edges, turn to the right side.

10 For ties, cut 2 pieces each 20 × ⅝in (50cm × 15mm) from floral fabric. Fold

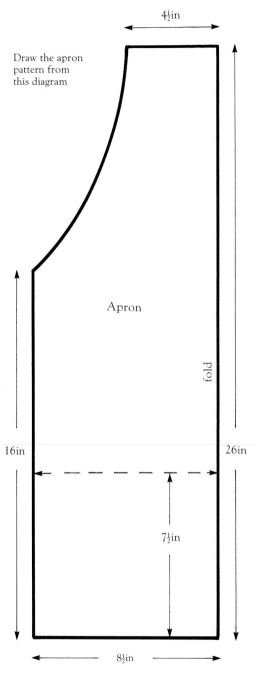

Draw the apron pattern from this diagram

4½in

Apron

fold

16in

26in

7½in

8½in

Making the apron

12 Turn under ⅝in (15mm) then 1in (2.5cm) on the top edges of the apron bib. Press and baste. Turn a double hem ¼in (6mm) along the armhole and side edges. Stitch. Stitch on the ties and neck strap. Bind along the top edge of the pocket with floral fabric. Press a ¼in (6mm) hem to the wrong side on the other pocket edges. Align the pocket with the bottom edge of the apron, matching the side edges, wrong side to right side of apron. Baste then stitch down the sides and across the bottom then lengthways into 4 equal divisions.

OVEN GLOVES

Preparation

13 On squared paper, draw a pattern for the glove section. Using the pattern, cut 2 pieces from striped fabric, 2 from floral fabric and 2 from wadding. From both striped fabric and wadding cut 2 pieces 32¼ × 6in (82 × 15cm). Place the glove pattern on the ends, mark round and cut out.

14 Baste the wadding to one piece of striped fabric. Quilt the entire oven glove with straight lines from end to end, spacing them ¾in (18mm) apart. Cut a piece of interlining to the shape of the oven glove, place on the wadding. Put the second fabric piece on top, right side out.

15 Working with the glove pieces, sandwich wadding between the fabrics and baste all round. Bind along the straight edges with striped fabric.

16 Hanging loop: Cut a strip of floral fabric 5 × 1½in (12.5 × 4cm). Fold in half lengthways right sides facing. Stitch the long edges. Turn to the right side. Fold to make a hanging loop.

each strap in half lengthways wrong sides facing and stitch the long edges. Turn to the right side.

11 Using the pattern, cut a pocket from striped fabric.

17 Place the glove pieces to the non-quilted side of the main oven glove section. Baste. Baste the hanging loop in the middle of one long side. Bind all round the complete oven gloves with bias-cut floral fabric strips.

Happy Christmas

Almost everyone loves a stocking that they can hang up at Christmas. The anticipation and excitement of prettily wrapped little gifts is all part of the joy. This festive-looking stocking will be treasured from year to year – and becomes part of the house decorations as well.

Materials

Red Christmas print fabric, 36 × 24in (90 × 60cm)

Green and white Christmas print fabric, 20 × 8in (50 × 20cm), for the cuff

Lightweight polyester wadding, 36 × 30in (90 × 76cm)

Green and red felt, 6in (15cm) squares

Gold Lurex ribbon, ⅛in (3mm) wide, 6¾yd (6m)

Double-edged lace, 1in (2.5cm) wide, 40in (1m)

Gold-edge white satin ribbon, ⅜in (9mm) wide, 40in (1m)

Green satin ribbon, ⅛in (3mm) wide, 2¼yd (2m)

Preparation

1 On squared paper, draw the pattern from the graph pattern (scale: 1 sq = 1in (2.5cm). Use the pattern to cut 4 stocking shapes from the red Christmas fabric (2 for the lining). Cut 2 stockings from wadding.

Making the stocking

2 Match the wadding pieces to the wrong side of the two main stocking pieces. Baste together. Pin the narrow gold ribbon in a lattice pattern over one stocking front, forming 2in (5cm) squares. Tie green ribbon bows and sew one to each intersection, catching the crossed ribbons together. '

3 Baste the stocking back to the front, right sides facing. Stitch all round, leaving the top open.

4 Baste and stitch the 2 lining stockings together, leaving a 6in (15cm) opening in one side seam.

5 From red fabric, cut a loop piece 8 × 1½in (20 × 4cm). Fold in half lengthways right sides facing and stitch, taking a ¼in (6mm) seam. Turn to the right side. Press. Fold and stitch to the top edge at the back of the main stocking.

6 Cut a piece of wadding half the depth of the green fabric cuff piece. Baste the wadding to the upper half of the cuff on the wrong side. Pin lace over the wadded part of the cuff, ¾in (18mm) from the top edge and again across the centre. Pin and stitch the gold and white ribbon centrally over the lace, anchoring it in place. Baste and then stitch the cuff into a ring. Fold in half, matching the raw edges, and baste to the top of main stocking.

7 Place the lining over the main stockings, right sides facing. Baste then stitch round the top edges, catching in the loop and cuff. Turn through the opening in the lining. Slipstitch the opening closed. Push the lining down inside the stocking.

8 Decoration: Trace the holly leaf and berry patterns. From green felt cut 6 leaves. Pin and baste together in pairs. Stitch all round, adding a small amount of wadding as you sew. Trim the seam allowance closely.

9 From red felt cut 2 berries. Work a gathering thread round the outer edges and pull up tightly round a small amount of wadding to form the berry. Fasten off the thread end. Stitch the leaves and berries to the cuff.

Trace the holly leaves and berry patterns

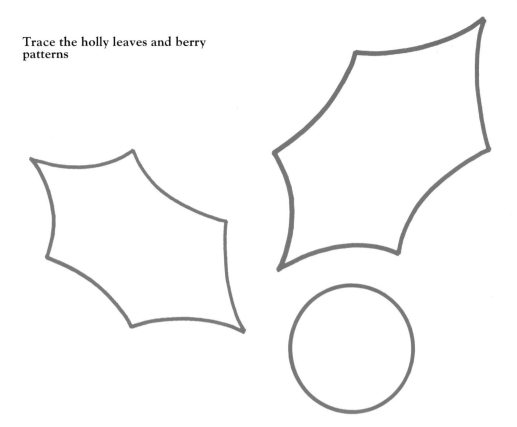

Bags of money

The Christmas stocking pattern can be adapted to make a charming and unusual advent decoration. Have the pattern reduced photographically so that the stocking is about 4in (10cm) long. Cut the shape from coloured felt (2 pieces for each stocking) using pinking shears so that a decorative edge is obtained. Sew two shapes together. On one side brush numbers 1–24 in clear glue and, before it dries, sprinkle glitter dust on the glue. If you like, the other side of the felt stockings can have a Christmas message spelled out in glitter dust letters, such as UNTO US A CHILD IS BORN, with a star on the last stocking. Make felt hangers for each stocking, sewing them into the back edge. Small sweets or candies can be placed inside or you might decide to make gifts of coins. Hang the stockings along a length of ribbon for a wall decoration, or fasten them to the overmantle. Alternatively, they could be hung on the Christmas tree.

Deck with holly

The trace-off holly leaves can be used for all kinds of Christmas fun. Cut them from card and use them as templates to cut shapes from green-coloured fondant icing for cakes. Use the shapes for making your own Christmas cards or for making leaf-shaped gift tags. Cut holly leaf templates from thin card and stencil red and green leaves on to white kitchen paper for an inexpensive giftwrap. Make a potato printing block by cutting a leaf shape into the cut surface and show children how to print holly leaves on to cards and invitations.

Christmas Stocking

Draw the pattern for the stocking on squared paper, scale 1 sq = 1in (2.5cm)

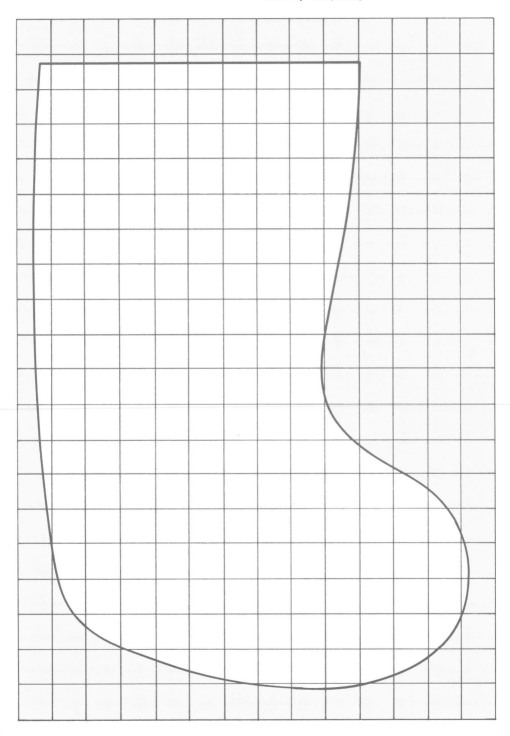

THREE

Better Techniques

❧

Most of the equipment that you need to make the items
in this book you will have in the home, while the remainder
are readily available from sewing counters in department stores
or from craft and sewing shops.

NO-SEW CRAFTS

Tools and equipment

Most equipment required for no-sew crafts is readily available, and you will have most of it already. There are a few specialist tools, however, which provide for greater creative possibilities, and help to give papercraft items a more professional finish.

The work surface is important. This should be at a good working height, flat and stable. You will require a protective surface to use over the work top, to protect it from cuts and scratches when using craft knives. A sheet of thick card or board is a suitable protection but should be replaced frequently as the surface will become pitted from successive knife cuts. It is worth investing in a special cutting mat. This has a surface which 'heals itself' after every cut, and thus remains smooth, and will not distort subsequent cuts made over it.

Cutting tools

You will need two kinds of craft knives: a heavy duty knife, like a Stanley knife or an X-acto knife, for cutting thick card, and a small knife, preferably a scalpel, for thin card and paper. Use straight blades, as these suit most tasks, and replace them often for the best results. Needless to say, these knives require care when in use. You should always cut straight lines by lining up the knife against a firm straight edge. Use a metal rule for this rather than a plastic or wood ruler, as these materials can easily catch in the blade.

You will need several pairs of sharp scissors. Have a pair of fairly small, easy-to-handle scissors with straight pointed blades for most cutting jobs, a longer broad-bladed pair for general cutting and stretching paper, and manicure scissors with curved blades for cutting round intricate shapes. A pair of tweezers is useful for handling small cutout shapes.

Other useful cutting tools are punches. Besides belt punches and stationery punches, wad punches can be used to punch holes through paper or card. These metal tools have removable punch fittings with different diameter holes. The tool is placed in position on the card or paper and struck smartly with a hammer to pierce the surface. Wad punches have the advantage over scissor style punches in that you can position them freely, and the size range of punch fittings gives flexibility for design.

Other equipment

Precise paper folding and creasing is important. One really useful specialist tool for marking fold lines on paper is a bookbinder's bone folder, which looks rather like a small modelling tool. This is drawn along against a straight edge and

Using spray adhesive

This very useful adhesive is ideal in projects which use giftwrap papers. An important advantage over other adhesives is its delayed sticking time, which means that sprayed papers can be re-positioned if necessary. Use spray adhesive to make thin papers more durable by laminating them to a thicker paper like cartridge paper. When laminating very small paper shapes, the spraying can be done with the paper resting on an expanse of newspapers. However it is best to make a spray booth from a cardboard carton, as this will protect surrounding surfaces and furnishings. Choose a carton large enough to comfortably hold the work for spraying.

Place a large box on its side and surround it with old newspapers. Place the card or paper shape as far inside as possible. To spray, hold the can upright and spray evenly over the surface with a sweeping motion. Handle the sticky work as little as possible when transferring it to the work surface. Lay the work sticky side up, and press the corresponding paper piece over. Smooth to stick, then trim round the shape as necessary. Turn over and smooth the surface flat.

leaves a gentle groove ready for folding. You can improvise, however, by using a knitting needle or a blunt, curve-bladed table knife, a letter opener or any other tool which creases rather than pierces the paper surface.

Mark fold lines with a bookbinder's bone folder

Drawing aids required include a pair of compasses, a set square and a ruler with small measurement markings, plus paper clips, and a stapler. You also need a pencil sharpener and a selection of HB and soft pencils, coloured pencils and felt tipped pens. A good quality eraser is essential.

Carbon paper is useful for transferring designs, but as the traced outlines cannot be removed, only use well-used carbon paper for tracings where the remaining outline does not matter.

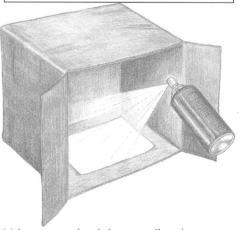

Make a spraying booth from a cardboard carton

To keep the nozzle of spray adhesive from clogging up after use, hold the can nozzle down and spray until the spray stops, then wipe over to clean the outside. If the spray has already clogged, wipe over with a cotton bud dipped in nail polish remover, then, if necessary, repierce the hole with a needle point.

Paints

Paints used for crafts include poster paints, acrylics, water colours and designer gouache. You can also use household emulsion paints and model maker's enamel paints, as well as multi-purpose metallic paint. Varnish for finishing and protecting work can be gloss, satin or matt finish. Use a varnish suitable for paper, or a household varnish applied to the previously protected surface (see below). Paint brushes should include a range of watercolour brushes, and small household decorating brushes.

A spray fixative can be used to protect finished work. This leaves a protective sheen on paper, making it less likely to mark or stain. Fixative can also be used on lightweight papers and paper printed on both sides – like magazine pages – to protect them from becoming transparent through over-wetting with glue or varnish.

Tapes and adhesives

Choose the right adhesive tape for the job. You may require transparent sticky tape, double-sided sticky tape, masking tape, or gummed brown paper tape. Specialist tapes like stretchy flowermaking tape (gutta tape) are available for binding wires and stems.

PVA is a multi-purpose, easy-to-use adhesive, which can be used both as a glue and a varnish. Although white, PVA dries transparent and gives a glossy protective surface. It can be used full strength or diluted with water. Clear, quick-drying and non-trailing craft glue (UHU) is a good multi-purpose adhesive for card and paper. Use a glue spreader for an even coverage. Stick adhesive (Pritt Stick) is required for some paper projects. This type of adhesive comes in a roll-up tube and is easy to control. An advantage is that unlike most other adhesives, it does not dampen the paper. Superglues are used to bond different types of material together. Use these for joining metal to paper for instance, as when attaching jewellery findings. One of the most useful adhesives, and probably the most widely used throughout the book, is spray adhesive. This allows you to laminate large or very small areas of paper together without stretching or dampening the paper. Spray adhesive should be used in a confined space to prevent the sticky mist settling on surrounding surfaces.

Checklist
Cutting out scissors
Small pointed scissors
Manicure scissors
Paper scissors
Craft knife
Scalpel holder and blade
Coping saw
Tape measure
Measuring stick
Metal edged rule and cutting board
Fabric marking pen
Tailor's chalk
Squared paper
Soft and hard pencils
Tracing paper
Latex adhesive
Spray fixative
All-purpose glue
PVA adhesive
Dressmakers' carbon paper, dark and
    light colours
Glass-headed pins
Assortment of needles for sewing,
    embroidery
Bodkin
Soft basting cotton
All-purpose sewing threads
Small press fasteners
Thin card for templates
Polyester toy filling
Watercolour paints
Poster colours
Modeller's enamels
Brushes and brush cleaner

Cutting paper and card

To cut thick card, lay it flat on a protective surface. Draw the pattern outline directly on to the card. Use a set square and ruler to check right angles and parallel lines. Line up the straight metal edge against the line to be cut. Press the craft knife against the metal edge, and firmly draw the knife towards you, keeping an even pressure on the straight edge to keep it still. Score the cutting line gently to mark it (and if only marking fold lines) then still with the straight edge in position, cut along the line again, pressing harder to cut through the card. To cut round curves, mark the shape lightly with the knife point, and cut round making sure that the free hand is pressing firmly on the card to keep it still, and that fingers are not in line with the knife, should it slip.

To use a scalpel on paper, follow the same basic process. When cutting small shapes with right angles and tight curves, start by piercing the corner point of each shape with the point of the blade, and cut away from the corner, drawing the knife towards you. This should ensure neatly cut points.

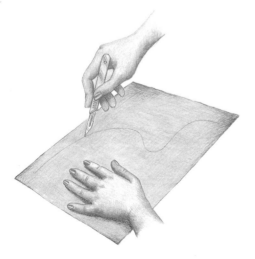

To cut round curves, mark the shape lightly with the knife point

REMOVING GLUES

Adhesive manufacturers will always help with advice about solvents for their products and some will supply these solvents direct if you write to them. In general, the first step in glue first aid is to scrape off any deposit and then proceed as follows:

Clear adhesive:
On skin, wash first, then remove any residue with nail varnish remover. On clothing or furnishings, hold a pad of absorbent rag on the underside, dab with non-oily nail varnish remover on the right side.

Epoxy adhesive:
Lighter fuel or cellulose thinners will remove adhesive from the hands. On fabrics, hold a rag pad under the glue stain, dab with cellulose thinners on the right side. On synthetic fibres, use lighter fuel.

Adhesive tape residue:
White spirit or cellulose thinners may do it. Or try nail varnish remover. Adhesives vary and you will have to experiment.

Latex adhesive:
Lift off as much as possible before the adhesive hardens. Keep the glue soft with cold water and rub with a cloth. Treat any stains with liquid dry cleaner. Scrape off any deposits with a pencil rubber.

If you are constantly using a tube of quick-drying glue for a project, choose a nail which fits tightly into the nozzle and knock it through a small piece of hardboard. When not in use, place the nozzle of the tube over the nail. This seals it temporarily and the glue is ready to use when you need it.

GLOSSARY OF TERMS

Canson paper
This is a textured art paper, used for pastel drawing. It comes in about 20 shades.

Cartridge paper or construction paper
This comes in different weights and qualities in white only. *Cover paper* which is a similar weight comes in several colours.

Ingres paper
This is a thin art paper with a texture of thin lines. Available in a good colour range.

Corrugated card (railroad card)
This is available in two forms. In one, the corrugated surface is open to one side. In the other, the corrugations are enclosed between two smooth surfaces.

Brown paper (Kraft paper)
Ordinary brown, good quality parcel wrapping paper.

Mounting card (mount card)
Available in 3 qualities, 4, 6 and 8 sheet, 4 being the thinnest. It is available in a range of colours, including black and grey, all with a white back.

Shiny card
This is like a thin mounting card but with a coloured, shiny surface.

Wad punch
This has a straight handle and punches of different sizes fit into the end. The punch is placed over thick card and the end is tapped with a hammer. It enables a hole to be accurately placed.

Stationery punch
These operate on a spring. Some can punch 2 holes and others a single hole.

Scoring
Breaking the surface of card or thick paper with a knife tip to enable a sharper fold to be made.

Cut straight lines aligning the knife against a metal rule

Working with felt
Felt is often used in no-sew crafts and has the advantage that it is colourful, inexpensive and very easy to handle. Usually, a template is recommended for cutting large shapes. Pencil or chalk round the template before cutting out with very sharp scissors. When cutting out small, fiddly pieces, it is a good idea to first mount the felt on to a sticky-backed label. Draw the shape on the paper and then cut out paper and felt together. This enables you to get a clean, sharp edge. Leave the paper on the felt when glueing the piece in place.

NEEDLECRAFTS

Materials and equipment

Cutting tools

Scissors: For basic sewing you need two pairs of scissors. A large pair for cutting out and a small sharply-pointed pair for snipping threads etc. Scissors must be sharp especially when cutting out fabrics. A good pair will give you clean, cutting lines rather than tearing the fabric.

Keep your scissors sharp. Most types can be sharpened on a kitchen knife sharpener. Never use dressmaking scissors for cutting out heavy paper or card because the cutting edge will be damaged, making the scissors useless for cutting fabrics subsequently. Avoid cutting across pins when cutting out as this can damage the blades.

For cutting out paper and card use a good pair of household scissors. For purely decorative purposes it is a good idea to have a pair of pinking shears, but do not use them for cutting out as they will not give an accurate outline. Pinking shears are also useful for trimming seam allowances to minimize fraying.

Measuring equipment

It is essential to have a good tape measure in your work box. This must be made from non-stretch material and have metal ends. The tape will be more useful if imperial measurements are marked on one side and metric measurements are marked on the reverse side. However, when working projects in this book, work entirely to the imperial or the metric measurements. Do not combine the two.

When cutting out large pieces of fabric you might find a wooden measuring stick useful. Here again they can be obtained with the two sets of measurements – imperial and metric.

Marking aids

From time to time you will need to mark the fabric with patterns and designs ready for cutting out. The easiest way to mark outlines on fabric is with a fabric marking pen or with tailors' chalk. Both pens and chalk come in a variety of colours, so choose one a shade darker than the fabric. The chalk will easily brush off the fabric and the pen marks can be removed by washing or, with some types, will disappear after 48 hours.

When you have to mark an appliqué or embroidery design on to fabric, use a sheet of dressmakers' carbon paper.

Sewing equipment

Pins: There is a good variety of pins on the market for different types of sewing. For most sewing, use a fine, standard length pin (but check to make sure that they are sharp). Blunt pins can snag the fabric, so discard these as you find them in the box. When working with some of the heavier craft materials use a thicker household pin, and if you are always dropping pins on the floor, buy glass-headed pins because these are easier to see against the carpet.

Needles: Needles are divided into groups, depending on their use. For general sewing use 'sharps', available in sizes 3–10 (the higher the number the finer the needle). If you prefer a shorter needle, use a 'between'.

When doing hand sewing, wear a thimble on the middle finger of the sewing hand. This will help push the needle through tough fabrics.

If you have a problem threading needles use a needle threader.

Sewing threads

One of the most important materials in a sewing project is the thread. Always match the type of thread to the fabric, such as silk with silk and cotton with cotton. For mixed-fibre fabrics choose an all-purpose thread. It is important that you match thread to the colour of the fabric. The various brands available all have good ranges of colours from which to choose and, as a general rule, you should go for one in a shade darker than the fabric. If you like to baste seams before stitching them, use a soft, loosely-twisted basting thread.

ENGLISH/AMERICAN GLOSSARY

English	American
Basting thread	Soft cotton
Bias binding	Bias strip
Buttonhole thread	Buttonhole twist
Latex adhesive (Copydex)	Latex adhesive (Slomans)
Cotton wool	Surgical cotton
Elastic bands	Rubber bands
Iron-on interfacing	Non-woven fusible interfacing
Polyester wadding	Polyester batting
Clear sticky tape (Sellotape)	Clear tape (Scotchtape)
Cartridge paper	Construction paper
Ruler	Yardstick

Fabrics

Before you start any project, look through your pieces store. You will probably find a remnant that you can use. When you are buying fabric for a dress or making a homesewing project, it is a good idea to buy an extra half metre. This, together with any off-cuts can often be put to good purpose, such as a set of matching accessories for a dressing table or some colourful items for the kitchen.

When selecting fabrics, remember that closely woven fabrics tend to fray less than loosely woven types. These fabrics are also easier to sew and generally give a good result. Make sure they have easy-care properties, so that they can be washed without the colours running and need little ironing.

Colours will be a personal choice, but when looking at a printed fabric, bear in mind the finished size of the project and avoid using large prints on small items. Most of the projects in this book will look best if they are made up in small sprig fabrics. The scale of checked and striped fabrics must be also noted; go for the small check ginghams rather than the larger versions whenever possible.

Interfacing

When a fabric requires extra body, use a layer of interfacing behind the fabric. Interfacing can be simply a layer of a thinner fabric, basted to the top fabric but fusible interfacings are easier to work with. Non-woven fusible interfacings can be bought in various weights.

Wadding (batting)

Wadding is the layer of fabric that is sandwiched between two other fabrics in quilting. Washable, polyester wadding comes in a range of different weights from light to an extra heavyweight (only used in upholstery). Use a lightweight wadding to give fabric extra body, and the medium and heavyweight versions for quilting, or when an extra layer for warmth is required.

To make diamond quilting even easier, there is an interfacing which is ready-marked with quilting lines. This is fused to the wrong side of fabric and then machine-quilting is worked over the marked lines.

Decorative trimmings

Small projects often look prettier with the addition of a decorative trim. Ribbons and braids come in most widths and the colour ranges are extensive so it is usually easy to find a good match. Besides plain ribbons in polyester satin, grosgrain, velvet and taffeta, there are printed ribbons, jacquard weaves and a variety of decoratively-edged ribbons to be found. Attach narrow ribbons and braids by stitching them down the centre. With wider ribbons, machine-stitch down both edges, always stitching in the same direction to prevent puckering.

Ready-made bias bindings are useful for finishing raw edges decoratively. These come in cotton or satin in plain colours and are also available in a pretty range of cotton prints.

Lace too comes in a variety of patterns and widths. Choose cotton laces if the item is to be ironed. Pretty broderie Anglaise is available flat or pre-gathered, some for insertion and for beading with ribbon. Some coloured laces are in the shops but if you need a touch of colour cotton lace dyes very easily.

Beads and sequins are lovely to work with and again the ranges of colours, sizes and types are extensive.

Fancy buttons can also be used as decorative trim, especially when they have a shank rather than central holes. Modern button ranges come in hundreds of different shapes – flowers, tiny animals and insects, ships, aeroplanes and steam trains, fun foods, initials, suns, moons and stars.

Other useful trims are ribbon flowers, which can be bought in mixed packets of different sizes.

PATTERN MAKING

Patterns are generally given in two forms, direct trace-offs and as graph patterns.

Direct trace-off patterns

To use these, you will need sheets of tracing paper or greaseproof paper. Lay the tracing paper over the book page and tape it down at the edges. Trace the image with a sharply pointed pencil.

Very simple shapes, such as squares or circles, may be drawn directly on to the wrong side of smooth fabrics, using either a soft pencil or dressmakers' chalk pencil. If fabrics are very thin and transparent, full-sized patterns can be direct-traced from the page, using a finely sharpened HB pencil or a coloured embroidery pencil. Another useful marking device is a pen which has air-soluble ink in it. After tracing a pattern the line remains on the fabric for a short time and, usually after sewing, it has disappeared.

Preparing patterns

Trace full-sized patterns on tracing paper, spacing pieces about an inch (2.5cm) apart. When a pattern piece is large, it may be split on the page and arrows or dotted lines will indicate where the pieces are to be joined. Trace the largest piece, move the tracing paper and trace the remaining section.

Some pattern pieces may be shown as one half only. To make a complete pattern, lay the folded edge of your tracing paper against the fold line on the master pattern (this will usually be marked 'place to fold'). Trace the outline, unfold the paper, refold and trace again.

Graph patterns

These patterns are given reduced in size on a squared grid. A scale is given and, to produce a full-sized pattern, you need squared dressmakers' paper marked with squares of the same scale. This paper is sold in large sheets, several to a packet, and can be obtained from dressmaking notions counters.

To reproduce a graph pattern you copy the lines on your pattern paper, square for square.

Transferring patterns

Patterns are transferred to the fabric with dressmakers' carbon paper. This is sold in sheets in packets of three or four colours, red, blue, yellow and white. A sheet is slipped between the pattern and fabric, and then the lines traced over with a tracing tool or an HB pencil.

Reading patterns

Before using a pattern it is important that you study the information given on it. This may take the form of words, numerals, letters, arrows and other symbols and is provided so that you cut out the correct number of pieces, arrange the fabric with the grain in the right direction and cut along folded fabric or from doubled fabric when required.

EMBROIDERY STITCHES

There are literally hundreds of embroidery stitches to choose from when you are decorating fabric.

Satin stitch

This is used for filling shapes. Work stitches evenly and so that they touch. Bring the needle through at A, insert it at B and bring it through again at C.

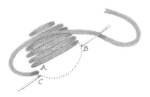

Straight stitch

Straight stitches can be used to fill shapes or singly. Stitches can also be worked in an eight-point star. Bring the needle through at A, insert it at B and bring it through again at C.

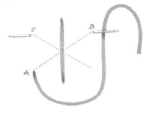

Back stitch

This stitch, properly worked, looks like machine-stitching and can be used for seaming. Bring the needle through at A, insert it at B and bring it out at C in front of A.

Stem stitch

This is often recommended for working flower stems and for outlining. Bring the needle through at A, the thread below the needle. Insert it at B and bring it through again at C.

Chain stitch

Bring the needle through at A and, with the thread below the needle, insert it beside A at B. The thread forms a loop. Bring the needle through at C, pull through gently, ready to start the next chain stitch.

Detached chain stitch

To work this stitch, from C, work a tying stitch over the loop.

French knot

French knots are a decorative stitch. Bring the needle through at A, wind the thread round the needle twice and then insert the point at B, close by A. Pull the thread through so that the knot tightens on the fabric surface.

SEWING STITCHES

Basting: This is a temporary stitch used to hold two layers of fabric together while the permanent stitching is worked.

Fasten the thread end either with a knot or with a double backstitch on the spot. Then take ½in (12mm)-long stitches through the fabrics. Once the main stitching is complete, snip off the end knot (or unpick the backstitches) and pull out the basting threads.

Running stitch: This stitch is used for gathering or when stitching fine seams by hand. Work from the right to the left. Begin with 2 or 3 backstitches on the spot. Pass the needle in and out of the fabric, making small, evenly-spaced stitches about ⅛in (3mm) long. When gathering, make sure that the thread is long enough to complete the area to be gathered.

Running stitch and gathering

Backstitch: This stitch looks like machine stitching when properly worked and is very strong and hard wearing. It is an ideal stitch to use when sewing seams by hand. Work from right to left. Begin with 2 or 3 stitches on the spot then work a running stitch and a space, take the needle back over the space, bringing it out the same distance away.

Slipstitch: This is a neat, almost invisible stitch that is used to catch a folded edge in place, such as when applying bias binding, or when joining seam edges from the right side. Work from right to left. Fasten the thread with a knot held inside the fold of the fabric. Bring the needle through and pick up a tiny stitch below the folded edge, then run the

needle through the folded edge. Bring the needle through and continue in the same way.

Working slipstitch

Herringbone stitch: This is a strong stitch used to catch 2 pieces of wadding together or to hold non-fusible interfacing in place. Work from left to right, always with the needle point to the left. Secure the thread just below the hem with 2 or 3 backstitches on the spot, bring the needle through and take the needle up diagonally across the hem and work a straight stitch from right to left, the thread over the needle. Take the needle down diagonally to the right, below the hem, and make another straight stitch. Take the needle up diagonally across the hem, and make a straight stitch.

SEAMS
Seam allowances
Always read through pattern instructions to check whether the pattern includes a seam allowance or if one is to be added when cutting out.

Rouleaux
Lengths of bias-cut fabric are made into tubing and then sewn into loops for fastening edges. Cut 1in (2.5cm)-wide bias strips into lengths plus ¼in (6mm) turnings at both ends. Baste the raw edges together with ¼in (6mm) seams, stitch the seam and then turn the tube right side out. Press only along the seam edge.

Pinning and basting

Many needlewomen pin pieces of fabric together and then start machine-stitching without basting. If you feel confident about doing this, by all means work in this way. Basting is helpful when complicated pieces are to be joined and helps you to stitch a straight seam. To baste, thread a needle with soft basting thread and knot the end. Work medium length running stitches just inside the stitching line, removing pins as you go. Finish with a backstitch. After stitching, unpick the backstitch, trim off the knot and pull out the basting thread.

Plain flat seam: Place the two pieces of fabric with right sides together. Pin and baste ⅝in (15mm) from the edge. Machine-stitch following the basting line, working a few stitches in reverse at each end of the seam to secure the thread ends. Press the seam open. Neaten the raw edges to prevent fraying with zigzag stitch. Alternatively the edges can be cut with pinking shears or can be bound with bias binding.

Right-angled corner: Stitch up to the corner then, with the needle still in the fabric, raise the foot and turn the fabric 90°. Lower the foot and continue stitching.

Sharp-angled corner: Work 1 or 2 stitches across the corner, before continuing along stitching the next side. Trim the seam allowance back round the point.

Curves: After stitching, snip into outward curves and cut small notches from inward curves. This enables the fabric to lie flat.

French seam: This self-neatening seam is very hardwearing. Place the 2 fabric pieces with wrong sides facing. Pin, baste and stitch the seam ¼in (6mm) from the edge. Trim the seam allowance back to ⅛in (3mm). Press the seam open. Fold right sides together, with the stitching

right on the fold. Press. Stitch again ⅜in (9mm) from the folded edge.

Wrong sides facing, stitch ¼in (6mm) from edge

Trim the seam allowance to ⅛in (3mm)

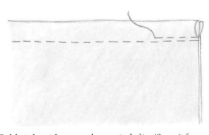

Fold right sides together, stitch ⅜in (9mm) from edge

Perfect curved seams
When sewing a curved seam, you will find that you get less drag and distortion on the seam if you start at the halfway point and stitch each side separately.

Flat-fell seam: A very strong, neat seam with a decorative finish. With wrong sides of fabric together, stitch on the seam line. Press the seam to one side. Trim inner seam allowance to $\frac{1}{8}$in (3mm). Press under the edge of the outer seam $\frac{1}{4}$in (6mm). Stitch this folded edge to the fabric.

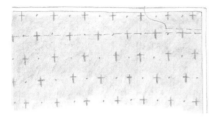

Stitch on seam line

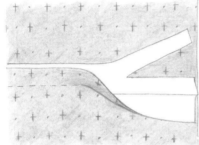

Trim inner seam allowance

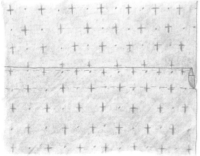

Stitch the folded edge down

FINISHING TOUCHES

Piping: Piping is a strip of bias-cut fabric, folded and set into a seam for a decorative finish. For a harder-wearing finish, such as on cushions, the piping covers cord.

Piping cord comes in several thicknesses for different applications. To estimate the width of the covering fabric measure round the cord and then add twice $\frac{5}{8}$in (15mm).

Bias strips: First, find the bias of the fabric. Fold over a corner of the fabric to meet the cut edge, the diagonal fold is the bias of the fabric. Cut through this fold. Use a rule and tailors' chalk to measure strips of the desired width from the diagonally-cut edge.

Pin, baste and stitch strips together along the straight grain ends.

Place the cord centrally to the wrong side of the fabric and fold the strip round the cord. Baste closely against the cord. With a piping foot on the sewing machine, stitch down the strip close beside the cord.

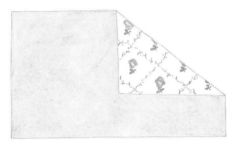

Fold over a corner to find the bias

Measure strips from the diagonal cut edge

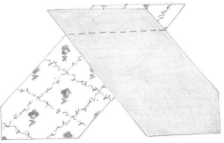

Stitch strips together on the ends

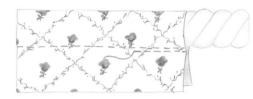

Stitch the fabric round the cord

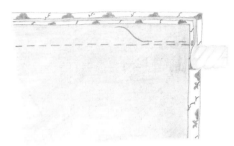

Stitch the covered cord between the fabric layers

Inserting piping: Baste the prepared piping between two fabric layers, matching raw edges. Stitch on the seam line.

Joining piping: Start stitching $\frac{3}{8}$in (9mm) from the end. When you come to the other end trim the cord to meet the first cord. Trim the fabric covering back to $\frac{1}{2}$in (12mm). Butt the cords, dab a touch of fabric adhesive to the ends so that they stick together. Fold under the trimmed fabric edge $\frac{1}{4}$in (6mm). Wrap over the starting end of the piping. Continue stitching.

Frills
Single frill: Decide on the finished width of the frill and add $\frac{1}{2}$in (12mm) for a doubled hem and $\frac{5}{8}$in (15mm) for the seam allowance. To estimate the length, measure along the place to be frilled and double the measurement. (If the fabric is very thick, only allow one and a half times the measurement.) Turn a double $\frac{1}{4}$in (6mm) hem along the bottom edge. Press and machine stitch.

Work 2 rows of gathering stitches along the top edge either side of the seamline. (If the frill is very long, divide the frill into equal sections and gather each section in turn.) Pull the gathers up

evenly to fit the main fabric. Pin then baste the frill to the main fabric, working across the gathering stitches to hold the frill in place. Stitch the frill in place. Remove basting threads. If the ends need to be neatened, work a double hem to match the bottom hem before gathering.

When making up a continuous frill, such as for a cushion, pin and stitch the frill strip short ends together into a ring before gathering.

Turn and stitch a double hem on a single frill

Work 2 rows of gathering along the top edge

For a continuous frill, stitch short ends together

Clever ways with ribbon
Polyester satin ribbon can be used for piping a seam. Fold 1in (2.5cm)-wide ribbon along the length, wrong sides facing. Pin and baste to the right side of fabric, matching the ribbon edges with the fabric raw edges. Place the second piece of fabric on top and stitch a $\frac{3}{8}$in (9mm) seam in the usual way.

Double frill: For a double frill, you need twice the required width and twice the seam allowance. Fold the strip lengthways, wrong sides facing, and baste

Baste and gather both layers together

Sewing tip

When instructions indicate that the seam allowance is to be added, first re-fold the fabric, right sides facing. Pin out the pattern. Draw round the outline of the pattern pieces using pencil or dressmaker's chalk pencil. (Add all marks etc.) Cut out ³⁄8in (9mm) from the pattern edge. Unpin the pattern. Baste the fabric pieces together, and stitch along the chalked line. This method enables you to achieve accurate stitching and perfect, straight seams.

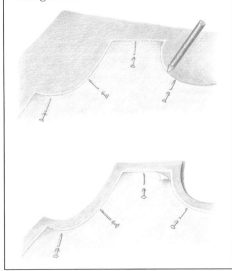

the raw edges together. Then gather and apply the frill as for the single frill, working both layers together. If you need to neaten the ends, fold the frill ends right sides facing and stitch across the ends. Trim the seam allowance and turn the frill right side out. Then gather and apply as for the single frill.

Binding edges

Bias binding is a neat way of finishing a raw edge as well as adding a touch of colour or pattern. Bias binding can be purchased ready-made in plain coloured or patterned cotton or in acetate satin. If you wish to make your own bias binding, cut bias strips (see page 108). Press the sides of the strips to the centre by one quarter.

To bind the edge of a piece of fabric, unfold one edge of the binding and lay against the fabric with right sides facing. The crease of the fold lies along the seamline. Pin, baste and stitch in the crease. Trim the fabric edge a little and fold the binding over the edge to the wrong side. Baste, then slipstitch in place, working over the previous stitches.

If the binding is to be topstitched, work the first stage of application in the same way. Bring the binding over the raw edge then baste and machine-stitch in place.

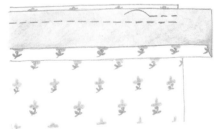

Open the binding and baste, then stitch, along the fold line

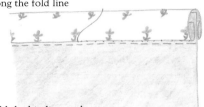

Fold the binding to the wrong side and slipstitch in place

Mitred corners

Mitring a turned-in edge: On a single hem, press under ¼in (6mm). Turn up the hem to the required length and press. Unfold and turn in the corner diagonally so that the diagonal fold meets the hem fold and press. Trim off the corner, leaving ¼in (6mm). Refold the hem over the trimmed corner.

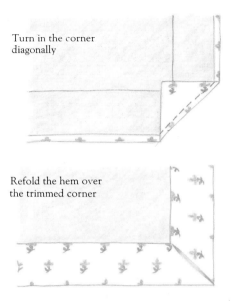

Turn in the corner diagonally

Refold the hem over the trimmed corner

Mitring a flat trimming: Place the trim against the fabric edge; pin and stitch in place up to the corner and fasten off. Fold the trimming back on itself, with the fold matching the next edge; pin firmly. Turn down the trimming along the next edge, pressing the diagonal fold that forms across the corner. Lift the trimming and stitch across the diagonal crease. Trim off excess and replace trimming. Continue stitching along the next edge. When all the corners have been mitred in the same way, stitch round the trimming along the inside edge.

Mitre binding: Unfold the edge of the binding and place against the edge, as explained before. Pin and stitch in the crease of the binding up to the seam line of the next edge, fasten off threads

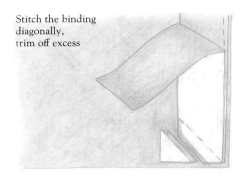

Stitch the binding diagonally, trim off excess

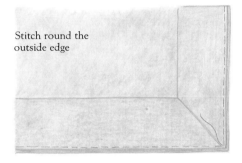

Stitch round the outside edge

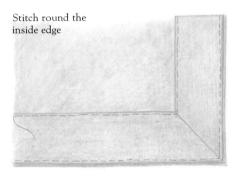

Stitch round the inside edge

securely. Fold the binding diagonally away from the fabric, aligning the binding edge with the edge of the next side. Pin and stitch again, beginning the stitching from the seamline. Take the binding over the raw edge to the opposite side, folding the excess fabric into a neat mitre. On the wrong side, tuck under the excess binding to form a neat mitre as well. Pin and slipstitch the remaining folded edge of binding in place, stitching across the mitre on each side, only when the binding is wide.

Acknowledgments and source list
The author and publishers gratefully
acknowledge the help of the following
companies:
Panda Ribbons, Stoke-on-Trent, UK, for
all the ribbons used in the projects.
Fred Aldous Ltd, Manchester, UK, for
clock hands and movement, joggle eyes,
animal squeakers and card mounts.

The projects in this book can be made
from a variety of easily obtainable
materials. A useful source of fabrics and
other home-decorating items is the
British-based company Laura Ashley,
whose range is widely available in the
USA. For details of where to find Laura
Ashley products in the USA, contact:

Laura Ashley
1300 Macarthur Bvd
Mahwah NJ 07430
Tel: (201) 934 3000